AF574087

I Couldn't Cry
When Daddy Died

I Couldn't Cry When Daddy Died

Iris Galey

SETTLE PRESS

I want to dedicate this book to my husband John,
my daughters Tony and Isy,
and my grandson Donat.

1988

Published by Settle Press
32 Savile Row, London, W1X 1AG

ISBN 0 907070 45 0

First published 1986
by Benton Ross Publishers Ltd
46 Parkway Drive, Glenfield, Auckland 10,
New Zealand

Cover design by Dexter Fry

Printed by Villiers Publications Ltd
26a Shepherds Hill, London N6 5AH

Here in our new country, many friends supported and helped me. They listened, encouraged, read, corrected and gave loving time and care.

I want to thank Cyril Hayden, Michael Morrissey, Yvonne Kalman, Jack Adlington, John and Pam Hall, Elizabeth Meldon, Mike Isles, Willow Macky, Daphne Calderwood, Hilda Phillips, Judy Knighton, Pat Wilson, Barbara Lucy Hosken, Barbara Whyte and Edith Hutchinson.

John and Kiira Sheppard, Brian Coote, Sue and Chris Dickie.

Les Harvey and Brian Brake.

Dr T. Gillespie, Heather McDowell, Sandra Butler, Renée, Eileen Swan, Miriam Saphira.

Ray Richards, Judy Hocquard, Ruth Hamilton, Sylvia Parker and Ross Markwick.

Jo Mayes, Tina Bareham, Dietlind Roots, Ivy Winterbottom, Miriam Arden, Gwen Coughlan.

Rob Wheeler, Alan and Lynda Stephenson, Bruce Logan, Graeme Packer, Anne Walls, Joanne and Grant Reid.

Dorothy, Douglas, Grant and Philip Moller, Gigi and Albert Sedlmayer, Judy and Peter Vucich, Esther and Philip Zimmerman, David Williams, Margaret (Tim), Diana and Hugh Fraser, Ruth, Peter and Stephen Lester, Norma and Adrian Spencer, Julia Butterworth, Gunilla and Selwyn Priest, Sue and Richard Norwood, Nan and Rick Norris, Ella Sandiford, Peter and Rochelle Faire, Joan Booth, David and Trudy Whittaker, Pam Bosch, Lynn McSweeney, Leanne and Wayne Silver, Elizabeth Worth, Margaret and Barry North, Margaret Mourant, Dave and Geerde Boss, Ariane Roelofs.

A special thanks to Mr and Mrs Wayne Noble of Mairangi Bay.

Thank you Helen Benton, Bob Ross and Joy Browne.

The biggest thanks go to my husband John and to my daughter Isy. Without John I could never have survived. Thanks to him I could become a whole person. Isy often had to be patient and understanding during the four years I wrote this book. Thanks to their help and co-operation I was able to write it. From time to time I found a note on my typewriter, 'Good writing, Mum. You're the best!'

Mother,

I can hear you saying that writing this book is in bad taste. Mother, I did not choose to write this book. This book wrote itself, as we are the sum of our experiences. It was the only way to find my identity, heal and remain sane. Now that it has been accepted, I am accepted. When I look into a mirror I see that there is a real person there. I have finally connected and become a real 'me'. In fact, writing this book as honestly as I could, is the biggest gift I could give to you, to my family and to myself and it was very, very painful. But now the pain and the unwanted intruding thoughts and negative feelings are gone. I am free and so should you be! I love you, Mum.

Olivia

Chapter One

Frau Dresden, our German housekeeper, offered me an apple after the funeral.

I couldn't stand the smell of Cox's Orange Pippins, because my father had blown his brains out, up there, in the attic where the apples were stored for winter.

I was fourteen and he had done it because of me.

I hated this house in Bradford, had hated coming home ever since we had lived here.

I looked round the scullery next to the kitchen and saw Frau Dresden lashing viciously at custard in a bowl. Her fleshy arms vibrated as she beat. She always made puddings in a time of crisis.

As I slurped the velvety yellow cream and looked across at the new red-brick fireplace, I missed the original black, polished Yorkshire hearth that had been ripped out. The only relic of old times left was the clothes-rack on a pulley and rope, hanging from the ceiling, with its damp forgotten washing.

Solemnly I regarded my father's underpants and the mammoth-sized ones of our housekeeper. I shuddered as an icy sweat drop slithered down my back.

I thought, he won't need those underpants any more. I was glad, and felt no sorrow. I wondered where Mummy was. Memories flooded back. . . .

Every evening when Father drove his Triumph Dolomite car up the drive, I was terrified. I would watch him through the side window. He'd proudly inspect his 'auto' for the slightest speck of dirt or dust on the glossy metallic-blue surface. I'd watch him limp in, dragging his arthritic hip through the back door. I'd hear him yell and criticise Frau Dresden.

Every evening he had me waiting there, to inspect shoes I had to clean. Sometimes he banged a shoe on to my head, other times he jabbed one into my middle.

'I taught her to cook and she never does it the way I showed her, and you're a blundering idiot too. Why are you too dumb to clean a pair of shoes the way I showed you? What a failure of a child I have! Why do I have to be cursed with such a collection of stupid females?'

He'd always shout back from the corridor, 'You've only got yourself to blame, you know! That's why you've got to be disciplined and brought up like this!'

Even if I did have lumps on my forehead, no one dared to question him. He had made it to the top. As a Swiss director of a well-known chemical company, he was greatly respected and feared. He had us all convinced that we were inferior beings. He would have much preferred a son and always gave the impression that he had to be pitied for the patience he needed to put up with us women.

But every night there had been worse, much worse. I could hardly breathe now, just to think about it.

'Not tonight! Not any night!' I said aloud, licking the custard bowl with my fingers and kicking my dirty shoes away.

'Vot's zat?' asked our housekeeper.

'Nothing, Frau Dresden.'

My thoughts returned to the funeral. I had tried hard to cry but the tears wouldn't come. We'd all stood around in front of the chapel in the cemetery. Mother told me my belt was twisted on my navy-blue funeral dress. I'd worn it to school for the day and was the only girl out of uniform. Now school was over for me. I remembered how I'd hoped that my hands, clasped behind my back, would make me feel and look more sorrowful than I felt. I walked into the chapel, glad to get away from the rows and rows of graves. Skeletons underneath. Rotting flesh. Grinning teeth into which dentists had once put gold fillings. All those nerves now dead. No drilling would be felt. I sat down in the front pew and was sure God could see my wicked thoughts instead of grieving ones.

I could see men from my father's company and friends. The ones I could see didn't cry. Nobody did but Mummy. The wreath from the firm was the largest there, all green and white and gold. Flowers that had pushed their way up through hard earth, after winter, to land on a coffin!

Now, home in the scullery, I wondered if I should have behaved differently to fulfil Mother's and others' expectations. I couldn't, I thought to myself. I couldn't because all I felt was incredible relief! The relief, now, was so great that I began to cry. . . .

'Thanks for the custard,' I called, and walked along the dark corridor, kicking the wood panelling.

'Stop zat, and pull your socks up!' shouted Frau Dresden.

I walked past the living room and was surprised to see no fire there. Every evening, after the shoe-cleaning routine it had been Father's habit to go and sit by the fire, his mug filled with malt Guiness beer. He would push the poker between the red-hot embers, and when it glowed as transparently red as they did, he'd quickly plunge it into the dark liquid and stir. I'd see the froth shooting up and over the rim, and him, sucking, his lips white with foam.

Once, feeling specially brave, I had asked, 'Daddy [for I was not allowed to call him Father], why can't you just simply love me? You know, like other daddies do. Not with . . . that . . . just love?'

He'd looked up with that mocking stare, the muscle in his cheek jumping. Rocking his knees apart and together, he then leaned back in the leather armchair, stretched his legs, put his hand in his trouser pocket, and said, 'Look at him bulging. Look at the bony-bony. Look how he's jumping! He's yours. He wants you to touch him and hold him. He can't help it! Look how your bony-bony jumps.'

I stood there, the horrible sick feelings rising inside, as always. I wanted to run away but I daren't. He leapt at me, grabbed my hand and pressed it there, quickly, looking to see if anyone was coming.

I turned away, after staring at the empty fireplace and the armchair where he'd sat. The same feeling engulfed me now. This sick 'aloneness' and 'worthlessness'. I ached all over, as always, for someone to hold me and stroke me, without that horrible part – that sexual part.

I walked on, then halted at the bottom of the dark staircase and looked up.

He had done it up there.

Slowly I began to make my way up to the attic. The smell of the apples enveloped me. Nauseating. I held out my arms over the banister, flapping them as if they were wings, and said, 'I'm a bird. I'm a bird and I can fly away and it's O.K.

to be a bird or a girl and to fly.' Why did I always say that when I walked upstairs? On the top landing I paused outside his bedroom door, the door through which I had been forced to go so often.

Timorously I pushed open the door. I stared up at the ceiling. 'It's all right now,' I said loudly. 'He's gone forever! He can't hurt me now, or ever again!'

After a pause I dared to look down. What I saw made me tremble. I didn't feel well, and I didn't want to stay, but I had to look.

On the striped blue-and-white mattress was a great fresh blotch. The scrubbed pink stain that signified the death of my father.

I made myself look around the room with the slanting roof and skylight. There was the desk, the stool, the bed and night-table – all black marble and chrome except for the red and white Swiss flag hammered on to the wall with four nails.

In my mind I saw the bony bald man as he had ripped my legs apart to kneel forcibly between them. I was nine when he started. I felt him strike as I squirmed. I saw him reach quickly for his gold-rimmed spectacles on his night-table, the better to peer at me, like the wolf-grandmother in Little Red Riding Hood.

Why did I have to think of that now? A fairy tale! Ugh! How he had rubbed and pulled and stared! How my thin arm hurt with cramp because of what he made me do. I had to go on and on and on, up and down, until he finally began to puff and pant. Disgusting – but the welcome sign for me to be permitted to go to sleep soon.

I said, 'They've thrown earth on top of you! You're weighed down now, securely nailed into your coffin! You can't ever hurt me or torture me again!'

I turned and ran all the way down those attic stairs for the last time.

I ran out of the house and across the road. I had only one friend in the world. I knocked.

I could hear Miss Abbott shuffling. She always peered through a crack in her dilapidated door, suspiciously asking, 'Who is it?'

'It's me, Olivia.'

'Oh, Olivia, my lovey.'

With this she opened wide her door, gazing upon me with an adoration that embarrassed me, as did the next part of her ritual greeting ceremony. She'd encircle me with her arms, slowly slither to her knees, pressing her ear down on my small form, until she seemed to be listening to my bony knees! I hated this part and felt uncomfortable, blushed, stifled a laugh, and wondered why on earth she always did this.

Then, as if to a secret signal, Miss Abbott suddenly gathered herself up with grandeur, and led the way into her living room.

I sank gratefully on to the bearskin that covered the settee and placed my hand on the huge head, feeling the yellow glass eyes. For the first time since the burial I relaxed, there in the warm glow of the fire.

Miss Abbott told me she lived withdrawn from the world. She was agoraphobic. She read through the nights and slept a lot during the day, but always had time for me. We had first met when she was feeding the birds in her garden.

Thanks to her I learned to know a vast range of English literature. I loved her to read to me and chuckled to myself when she read *Great Expectations* because it seemed to describe exactly what I saw around me in her ancient house. The curtains were torn and threadbare, the wallpaper shredded and faded, and sugar crusts stuck to unwashed teacups. This all had a strange appeal, in contrast to our Swiss perfection brought about by constant nagging and scrubbing, unrest and frustration.

I loved it here. Father had forbidden me to come, but now I was free to have friends. Sitting there, after the funeral, this suddenly sank in. Also the realisation that the beatings, the cruelty and degrading injustice from my father were all over.

I looked at Miss Abbott's gentle face, at the worn, moss-green overall she wore year in and year out, and at her hair in two greying plaits. It all seemed lovely and safe. As I began to unwind, I suddenly knew that this safe feeling here, with this new person in my life, was something that I had never known with my own people. I wondered about Mummy and pushed away the comparison.

I looked at the piles of books everywhere, the oil paintings in heavy gold frames and the cases of stuffed birds with the ostrich egg I was sometimes permitted to cradle in my hand.

'I'll get you a cup of tea and your cho-co-late biscuits,' she'd say.

I would answer, 'I love the way you say cho-co-late' and she'd go on with, 'And I love the way you say Seal-y-a-ham dog.' And we'd laugh together. Me, because of her very English accent, and she because of my Swiss accent.

Now I asked her if she'd read the 'Balcony Scene' to me, or 'To be or not to be', but then I decided that putting it off wouldn't make it all go away and that I needed to talk. I needed her to confide in, to try to understand what it had all been about.

'I'd like to talk to you, but I don't know how.'

'I understand. I like your navy-blue dress. It's so much nicer than black.'

'They buried him today. I couldn't cry.'

She just said, 'Lovey.'

Silence. After a while I said, watching every muscle in her face, 'He shot himself.'

Nothing in her face moved in a bad way. I relaxed a bit more. I had to talk, had to get it out.

'He did it because of me.'

I felt as cold as a stone.

'You can tell me everything, but only tell me about it if you want to, deary. Only if you find it helps. I've known a long time that there was something wrong, lovey. You always seemed so burdened.'

'It's hard to talk and it's all so . . .'

'There, there, it's all right. You're all right. A good cry will do you the world of good.'

I blubbered, 'It's as if all the hurt wants to get out . . . out by words . . . but Mummy says it's too shocking. I'm not supposed to talk about it. But I had to do it with him and that wasn't too shocking, was it, for me to suffer through? Oh! I only spoke twice about it, because I couldn't stand it any more. Once to those visitors who got the police, and then to the policewoman.'

'Shush, shush, lovey. Here's a hanky.'

'I just wish I could understand it all, why he did it all. You see, he did these terrible things to me and said it was all normal but one may never talk about it. I'm so confused and I just don't understand. . . . And when I spoke, when I just couldn't stand it any longer, bang, he dies, shoots himself, and it's all my fault and I can't even cry at his funeral and I couldn't love him. . . . Sorry, yes, sorry for him, bedause he limped and had such pain, always, but oh, he was so mean at times! Never a daddy, never a family. . . .'

She drew me close, putting her arm round my shoulder, and I sobbed like never before.

'It's the only family I have, I had . . .' I howled, 'and I suppose it's better than having no family at all.' I sobbed on and could hardly breathe.

'There, there, dear. I had no idea . . . it's just too terrible what he did to you. To think you suffered so, were so terribly unhappy, right under my nose, and no one knew.'

'He was so strict and did it all under the threat of murder.'

'Olivia!'

'If you knew it all, you wouldn't like me any more. You wouldn't want to be my friend. I know it. I know.'

'Olivia, of course I'll always like you, and be friends. It's just such an incredible shock! To think that no one knew and could help you! What on earth did he do to you and how long for?'

'For four years.'

'Oh, my poor, poor child. Oh, I'm so glad it's over . . . I mean . . . What on earth did your mother say? Didn't she know? Couldn't she . . . ?

'That's what the policewoman asked. Mummy didn't know. She was so frightened of him, too. We all were.' I drank my cold tea and ate a biscuit. Talking about it feels like a revenge. Is that fair?'

'Olivia, if grown-ups, who should have taken good care of you and were responsible for your wellbeing, have done something to upset you so much and hurt you so deeply, then anything's all right for you to do to help you cope, now and in the future. You have rights too, you know.'

'There's so much I don't understand.'

'I'm so angry, child. Look at you! Small, thin and pale. Always looked like an underfed fledgling. How dare your parents treat you like this! To think you were so helpless, so much at his mercy.'

Her anger seemed to give me strength and I wanted to get it all off my chest. So I began.

Chapter Two

'It all started about four years ago.

'It seemed to begin with the talk about piano lessons. You see, I wanted a bicycle more than anything in the world. A lovely dark-green one with chrome that shines. (Horse-riding had always been my heart's biggest wish, but Daddy – I mean my father – would never have permitted that.) One morning at breakfast, around my tenth birthday, he asked me if I wanted a bicycle or piano lessons. I was so thrilled! I beamed and was just going to say "A bike" when I saw my mother's eyes. You know, that look that only a mother can give you. She loved Mozart and was homesick for Switzerland and always told me how music in the house would help. I felt so sorry, for the sadness in her eyes, so I said, "Piano lessons."

'Afterwards I thought that it always seemed bad of me to want something for myself, and I puzzled over it, because I only seemed to be a good girl if I chose and did and behaved and thought as they wanted me to. As if I didn't matter or was too unimportant or real to have ideas of my own. Somehow this all seems to belong to it. I don't know why, though. I'm all confused.

Anyway, after this breakfast talk about bikes and piano lessons, Father said it was time he told me the "facts of life". To Mummy he said, "Leave it to me, Ida. She's old enough now," and took me into his study.

'After he closed the door he began to talk about flowers and pollen, seeds and bees. I felt uncomfortable among the heavy dark leather furniture, which was clammy cold against my bare legs. He said that I had eggs in my tummy, millions of them, and he, like all men, had seeds. "Little wiggly things," he said. He then told me that soon I'd have blood coming out of me and would smell and be messy. "Never let anyone notice, or be unclean about it," he snapped, as if I'd done something badly wrong.

'I didn't know what he was talking about and it made me frightened. The rest, he said, he'd show me later, himself. The way he said that, and the way he looked, made me feel threatened . . . uneasy.

'I was allowed to go then, to clean the car, as I had to every Saturday while children rode up and down the street on their bikes. Father never permitted me to join them.'

'Soon after that talk, one night, he came to my bed.

'He must have touched me . . . down below, because I woke up feeling queer, as if I'd wee-wee-ed, wanted to, or something. I had such a shock. But he pressed me down and whispered in my ear. He said I had to listen carefully as this was very important.

'For a minute, his whispers, moist in my ear, sounded like schoolgirl secrets. The closeness would have been lovely if it had been a friend or Mummy. But he was saying how he would teach me things young women should know, not to be such "lousy" wives and lovers. That it had to be a secret thing between him and me. I was never to mention it to anyone, not even to my mother. Then he mentioned his pistols – he often made me practise shooting at targets in our cellar – and now he said he'd have to silence me if I talked. . . . Miss Abbott, it's so hard to go on.'

She put her arm round me. I wanted to get it all out because I'd learned so many 'rights' and 'wrongs', and was so mixed up.

'He said this was the way things were always going to be, even later when I was married. He knew I was frightened of the dark and of the ghosts he saw in our house, so he said if I was a good girl and did everything he wanted me to do, I would come to no harm. I'd do anything not to make him angry, but he insisted it was my fault, because I was so stupid and so he had to punish me and hurt me a lot. I was always scared of him.'

Miss Abbott looked into the fire and gently stroked my back.

Now that this was out, I drank some more tea.

'Didn't you ever have fun with other children or time to play?'

'Father liked to keep me isolated. That's why he wouldn't let me come here, either. Mummy took me to films when he was away and took me to birthday parties and invited her arts-club friends. If she was away too, Frau Dresden was quite nice. In the evenings there was homework, piano practice and the dishes. And when he was home, the walk!'

'What's so terrible about a walk?'

'With Father, everything was spoilt.'

Reluctantly I began to tell her about the nightly walks with him on the nearby Yorkshire moors. Up there, where usually I loved to run in the sun and the wind with Glen, my dwarf Scotch terrier, feeling so free and happy, looking across miles and miles of patterns the dry stone walls made of the dales and moors. Glenny would be barking and sniffing for rabbit hide-outs while I lay on the turf, breathing in the fresh warm scents as I watched the skylarks dart and dive.

But every night he'd first stand over me and my schoolwork. He made 'tit, tit, tit', hissing sounds between his teeth, while drumming with three fingers, like a horse galloping, waiting for my answers to questions he'd popped. Arithmetic or French. It would be tit, drum, question, clout on the ear, question, clout, drum, tit! He made me so scared I couldn't think, and I could have screamed and been sick every time. Especially when he suddenly said, "Walk!"

'He would limp up the hill, Miss Abbott, and he'd make me put my hand into his raincoat pocket that wasn't really a pocket but a slit, and he made me touch him . . . his . . . you know.'

I looked down at the bearskin rug.

'I could have been sick every time. I kept on looking up at the stars and wondering if God would want me to have to do all these things I hated so much and how long I'd have to do them for. At school and on Sunday they taught us to honour and respect and love our parents.'

'My goodness, my poor child!'

'Oh, Miss Abbott, it got worse. Some nights I'd have to kneel down behind a stone wall, up there, and take it in my mouth. He got rough. That nearly choked me and he'd hold me by the ears or hair, moving me back and forth like a sheep being shorn. I'd make little sob noises. He sucked in air through his teeth, making an F-sound and when the F's got shorter and louder I knew he'd be finished soon.'

Miss Abbott was crying.

'He got very angry when I didn't want to swallow the . . . the white stuff.'

'Olivia! Oh, Olivia, he was a sick man! Your father was a very, very sick man!'

'That's what the policewoman said.'

'Stop crying, love. Dry your tears. Not with your sleeve. Here's a hanky.'

I blew my nose and went on.

'She . . . she was the second person I had to tell it all to, after Mummy and the men at dinner who went to the police. But she made me tell it several times, right from the beginning, over and over again, as if she didn't believe me.'

'She had to, deary, becaue some people make up stories like that and she had to be sure it was true. It must have been an ordeal for you. Was she nice? Was she kind?'

'Oh, yes. A bit grand in her uniform but ever so kind.'

'How did all this suddenly come out into the open?'

I told her how glad I'd been when Father had had to go away for three months to get treatment for his arthritis, on the Isle of Ischia. How wonderful it had been not to have him bothering me. No hitting, scolding or punishing. I could go to bed and sleep the nights through in peace. It was a new life, freer and happier, with only a few bad dreams.

'Then, one evening, Mother had two Swiss men from my Father's company to dinner. During the meal she suddenly said, "Olivia, I've had a letter from your father. He's coming home tomorrow."

'I was stunned, then terrified. I knew it would all be the same again. All that violence and those nights and the horrible mornings in the bathroom, the pain, the troubles and fear, the Saturdays . . . and I heard myself crying out, "No! Never again! I don't care if he kills me. I never want to see him again!"

'They all stared at me, their mouths open and questions in their eyes. So I told them all, told them what he'd done all those years.

'Mummy went white. She just stared at me, unbelieving. She got up and said with a funny, wobbly voice, "It can't be true. I didn't know. I didn't know anything. It can't be true." On and on.

'One of the men left the table instantly and the other man ran after him. They soon returned with Miss Killarney, the policewoman.'

Miss Abbott looked at me and said, 'How could your mother not have known?'

'That's what they all asked. But you see, Mummy isn't well. She paints all night in the basement, and drinks whisky and smokes, trying to forget how homesick she is. In the daytime she sleeps. Frau Dresden takes care of everything. . . .'

'I feel terrible.'

Miss Abbott stroked my hair.

'I loved coming here and it helped. I wonder what's going to happen to me, now. D'you know, I always felt sorry for my father because of his pain in the hip and the limp, but if it hadn't been for his arthritis he'd probably still be here and. . . .'

'Hush, lovey, hush! It's all over. Do you think you'll stay in England?'

'I'd love to. Specially now. I love Yorkshire and I'd even be allowed to eat fish and chips now. He never let me be like other children.'

'Fish and chips? That doesn't seem such an extremely desirable delicacy to yearn for!' Miss Abbott laughed.

'It does to me . . . because it would make me feel like one of the others . . . one of the crowd.'

'I think I know what you mean.'

'I do hope everything's still all right. After what I've told you, I mean.'

'Of course everything's still all right and it always will be, between us, Olivia. You just come over here whenever you want to. Are you feeling a bit better?'

'Oh, yes! I just feel a little strange, like when you sprain your ankle, but it's as if I've sprained my heart, or soul or whatever it is that's inside.'

'I know the feeling. Time is a great healer. You'll grow and get over it all.'

'Miss Abbott, am I a bad person because I couldn't feel sad at the funeral?'

'No. You feel what you feel and if he wasn't a person to leave you memories worth missing, and crying for, why should you feel sad?'

'That almost sounds as if it's nicer to have bad parents because then you don't miss them so much as you would if they'd been loving.'

'No, child, no! It's not good not to be missed, or loved, or worth remembering. I hope you'll remember me.'

With this she clasped me to her and held me close.

Smiling up through my tears, I said, 'Isn't it lovely? I won't have to sneak in here in secret.'

'Lovely! Go on then, child, run along.' We walked out of the door. 'And remember, you're lovely yourself. You'll make your way.'

As I started to walk towards her gate I looked across the road, over at our black stone house. I stopped and looked back at my friend standing in her doorway. I suddenly had to turn and run back to her.

I clung and we sobbed openly.

Chapter Three

I turned and walked across the road, up the stone stairs past the roses and into the house.

The hissing of the iron and the damp, steamy odour of fresh washing was a smell I always associated with other people's happy homes.

'Is Mother home?' I asked Frau Dresden.

'Is Mozer home! Is Mozer home! Always zat question.' She shrugged me off as I tried to give her a hug.

We had something to eat together in silence, and later I went up to bed. After trying to concentrate on *Just William*, because it usually cheered me up, I put out the light, disappointed with the evening at home, even though Father wasn't there to worry me.

To the ticking of my tiny Swiss alarm clock, I relived and relived every second of the last few amazing days.

I felt a bit better about telling Miss Abbott and about the way she had reacted and spoken to me. But I hadn't been able to bring myself to tell her about the worst part, about the horror of him killing himself.

I turned round in the dark. I was hot. I hated remembering. The fear still made my flesh creep and I wanted to forget, but everything kept flashing back in pictures.

Miss Killarney didn't seem to be able to believe me, at first. To many doubting questions I'd answered that if I didn't obey, he'd pull my ears till they bled where the lobe joined the cheek. (She'd looked and saw how dry and flaky the skin was there.) I had also told her how I never got enough sleep and would often faint during assembly and prayers in the school hall. They found out that I had low blood pressure, migraines that made me sick, raw, sore hands and chilblains, boils, shingles and much thick discharge. In the mornings he'd make me sit in the wicker chair in the bathroom. He stuck my legs out under the arm-rests, right and left, and would sit in front, on the floor, and stare and fumble. He beat me into this position, grazing my legs, till I sat as he wished me to.

Miss Killarney had again said he was a sick man and that she was very sorry about what had happened to me. That had made me cry.

She had gone on to tell us, Mummy and me, that the following evening we would have to go to the railway station to meet the train, as if nothing had happened. We were to tell him that I'd been having nightmares and that Mother was sleeping in my bedroom. She said that the police would talk to him and take him to hospital where he could be treated and healed. . . .

I tossed.

Seeing him at the train station the next night had reminded me of the time I had first met him five years ago, in Basel, after the Second World War. I lived through it all again as we stood at the station, waiting for him, the day after I'd told Miss Killarney.

I saw him first.

The one man in the crowd limping. Falling slightly to the left, he still dragged his leg.

The circle of bald patch under the French beret had grown larger. The gold-rimmed spectacles sat on flakes of dry skin, peeling after sunburn. His limp still struck pity in me, like a match striking a matchbox.

I smiled up at his sneer too eagerly. I blushed crimson.

He kissed us all dutifully.

As soon as Mother went in search of a taxi and Frau Dresden helped the porter, he turned to me.

'Whom have you told?'

'No one, no one,' I lied. Then blurted out immediately, under his waiting gaze, 'Mother sleeps in my room, because I still have nightmares.'

Instantly I knew that I'd fallen into the first trap. I knew that I'd given everything away.

We drove home in tense silence. As it was late, I excused myself and went straight to bed, waiting, panic-stricken, until Mother slid between the sheets in my room.

In the morning, petrified, I begged Mother to come into the bathroom with me. At breakfast he said he would drive me to the school bus stop. I couldn't swallow. He saw me look at Mother. Was no one going to come with us?

I couldn't believe it when I had to get into the car with him.

Mother, for once up at this hour, waved, her pale blue eyes wide, her short black hair untidy for the first time.

He sped away but didn't take the usual route.

Why had Mother and Miss Killarney let me down? Why this? What was he going to say, to do to me? Wasn't anyone coming to help?

I was going to be late for school. Where was he taking me?

As I looked at him from the side, I thought his dark tan made him look more threatening. I daren't keep my eyes on him. I stared in front of me, frightened out of my wits, my heart racing.

'Who did you talk to and what did you tell?'

'I don't know what you're talking about.' I giggled and stopped.

He drove on in silence, speed mounting. And suddenly I knew. I felt all colour and warmth drain from my body. He was driving towards 'suicide edge'. The one place he had talked about so often. The place where there was a sheer drop, off the highest level on the moors, at Malham.

I was right.

There was nothing I could do or say. From bitter experience with him, I had learned that I never had any power or chance to stop horrific things from happening. I knew that this time it would be the end.

Why do other kids have such nice daddies, I thought.

Off the main road, on to the moors he sped, out towards the edge. I contemplated jumping out, but my mind and limbs were lame. And, anyway, at this speed I couldn't get out. And even if I did manage it without killing myself, he'd catch me. There was no place to run to or hide.

He raced on. His eyes were unblinking.

It'll be quick. It'll be over quickly. It won't hurt.

I closed my eyes.

He swerved.

Without one word or glance in my direction, he turned the car and headed back.

I dared not relax or be relieved, for I was sure he had something worse in store, but he drove me straight to the bus stop. I was late and would be punished at school. What would I say?

I jumped out of the car the second it stopped.

He didn't drive off. He just sat and stared, as I waited there, shivering, trying to avoid his eyes. I even made a feeble attempt to smile. Then, gratefully, I scrambled on to the top of the double-decker bus as soon as it drove up.

At school I was summoned to the headmaster's room. I was still too shaken even to think. He didn't question me about my late arrival but informed me that there had been a phone call to tell me to go straight to the Rosenbergs' house after school.

I breathed a sigh of relief, hoping to be spared any further confrontation with my father. I was so grateful for the way the onrushing terror and tension of that morning had suddenly come to an end that I refused to pursue the possibilities of its outcome. I dared not even ponder on the whys!

Herr and Frau Rosenberg, friends of the family, informed me that my mother and father were expected for dinner and that I was to stay the night. No explanation was given. I was puzzled, as this had never happened before.

Ill at ease, we sat in the living room until my parents arrived.

After drinks were served, Mother spoke.

'Olivia has been practising the *Ave Maria* while her father was away. Wouldn't it be nice if she could play it for us? You've played it so well at home. I'm sure it's time for you to give a first little performance. I'm sure we'd all enjoy it.'

She'd never done anything like that before. I didn't think she'd noticed my improvement. Nervously I got up.

'I've never played to people,' I said.

Frau Rosenberg, who was the fattest and most relaxed person I knew, laughed reassuringly and said, 'There's no time like now, to begin. Go on, give it a go. You can only try to do your best and if that includes mistakes, that doesn't matter in the least. Just try.'

So I sat down at the piano and played.

I got through, happy not to have made one mistake.

'Excellent! Very musically played. You're very gifted,' Frau Rosenberg said, as she got up and left the room to attend to dinner.

As I turned round on the piano stool, I saw tears running down Father's cheeks.

I stared in utter amazement.

I looked quickly at Mother.

She too was silently crying.

Herr Rosenberg was filling the glasses and hadn't seen them. I watched them both stealthily wipe their faces with the backs of their hands.

Then they all talked of trivial things.

As I once more tossed and turned in bed, my heart ached. Suddenly I realised that that was the last memory I had of Father. Father crying!

The next day I was once more summoned to the headmaster's room.

'You are a busy girl, aren't you? I've had another phone call for you today. I'm to tell you that you're to go and stay with Val Arnolds after school.'

The way he looked at me, I felt he expected an explanation, but I was at a loss for one myself.

Mrs Arnolds was as surprised at my visit as we were. Nevertheless, she made me welcome and spoilt us with a wonderful Yorkshire meal.

To me, Val was the luckiest girl in the world. She had a lovely family and a horse of her own. She lent me some jodhpurs and, feeling absolutely exhilarated, I ran across the fields with her in the direction of her pony. A shrill whistle stopped us.

'Darn it! It's Mum's "come home" signal,' Val cried.

As we ran back we could see our mothers and Miss Killarney standing in front of the house. Before I reached the group, the policewoman came towards me. I saw that Mother was crying.

Miss Killarney put her arm round my shoulder and led me away down the gravel path. 'Now, Olivia, you're going to have to be very brave,' she started. And instantly I knew. Knew that my father was dead. Everybody was going to expect me to be sad and sorry and cry like people did when somebody died.

She said, 'Your father is dead. He has shot himself.'

I wondered if it was decent to feel so relieved.

I couldn't burst into tears. I felt incredibly free.

I looked up at Miss Killarney, looked down because I nearly had to laugh, looked back and said, 'How terrible.'

I walked back to Mother and put my arms around her.

I thought, I can't pretend to cry.

My head felt funny. Shouldn't Mother be putting her arms around me? But I don't feel guilty for telling . . . I feel deeply sad because I feel absolutely nothing for him.

I saw the small group standing around. Somewhere, someone was calling to hens. The responding clucks pecked at my brains.

Mother was looking at me with her pale blue eyes full of dead-fish tears! I closed mine and wished everybody would leave me alone. I was so terribly tired, and torrents of saliva seemed to be gushing from nowhere into my mouth.

Mother said, 'Give your watch to Val.'

Battling with all the spit in my mouth, I asked, 'Why?'

'For a farewell gift,' she said.

I was proud of my watch and didn't want to give it. . . .

I opened my eyes long enough to look at my watch with the red second-hand jumping. It suddenly leapt away from the numbers, pointing at me, piercing my eyes as I was drowning, swallowing, choking. . . .

I tried to steady myself . . . mustn't show how I feel . . . mustn't scream . . . must be a good girl . . . poor Mummy . . . must go and hold and comfort her and say I'm so sorry. . . . If only I wasn't so deathly tired.

'Olivia! Olivia! Olivia!' They were all shouting my name when I woke up. From somewhere a friendly Yorkshire voice floated up to me.

'Eee, thank God you're better, luv.' It was Mrs Arnolds stroking my cheek. 'Have you ever fainted before? Eeh! You did give us a turn, ducky.'

Mother started talking in a rush. 'She has low blood pressure and can't stand for long.'

Mrs Arnolds was propping me up, spooning strong, sweet tea into my mouth. When I had first come here she'd smiled, like now, and said, 'Whenever someone comes into this house t'kettle goes on t'stove.' She knew from Val how I loved tea.

As I looked down I saw that my wristwatch had gone. Val was holding it and looking at it in her hand.

'Can I really have it?' she asked uncertainly.

'Yes, of course,' my mother said. 'We've given you so much trouble.'

Soon after that we left.

Miss Killarney drove us home. I was surprised to see that Duckworth Lane still looked the same. Surprised to see people behaving as if nothing special had happened.

A little boy was peeing off the pavement into the gutter. The sight of this made me throw up. Miss Killarney stopped the car. I opened the door and couldn't stop retching.

Mother apologised for me.

Looking to see what time it was later that evening, I felt much worse about the loss of my watch than about the loss of Father.

Mother and I never ever talked about what had happened. Not about all that Daddy had done to me. Not about the suicide. He was there one day and gone the next. Just like that! As if he and our 'family life' in England had never existed.

Chapter Four

For the last time her weighty bulk, on dwarfish cylinder legs, stomped down our stairs. Frau Dresden was leaving us. Chappy, the Old English sheep dog, went with her. They left a surprisingly painful gap.

We never had any meals in that house from then on.

Mother seemed to look upon pubs, cafes, tearooms and restaurants as substitute 'homes away from home'. We spent hours there. She, smoking and drinking whilst writing letters, telling me not to disturb her. Me, sitting and waiting. Mum smiling up at me from time to time, breathing a faint, 'Ach Gott! Ach Gottchen!'

We were often invited for meals by friends.

The only place in which I really felt at home was the Clarks'. I'd met them because of the fog. Whenever it grew too thick for my hour's bus trip from Bradford to Ilkley, I was allowed to stay at their small red-brick bungalow with the bay windows. That's why I loved the mist and the fog, even when it was so dense that men with lanterns and horns had to walk in front of cars and buses. The Clarks' home had a warm, friendly atmosphere. Gladys Clark possessed the broadest Lancashire dialect, coupled with a delightful sense of humour. To her I'd be 'luv' and 'ducky' and 'me darlin'.

Then Elly Zimmerman arrived. Just as when, at times of crises, Frau Dresden used to make puddings, my mother could always make an aunty or uncle appear on these occasions. They popped up like rabbits out of top hats. They'd be willing and convenient as long as Mother needed them, only to disappear again for years, until she waved her magic wand. There was always someone or someplace for me. I hated this.

The minute I saw this aunty I knew two things for certain. One, Frau Dresden had been fantastically fat, and two, my mother was truly incredibly beautiful. I also sensed the threat of a new separation.

Up to that time, I had seemed to sit around waiting. The sudden absence of Father and all the horror concerning him had come too abruptly. I seemed to sit lame and stunned, too surprised and insecure to continue feeling relieved. It even seemed strange not to hear his car motor. Strange not to have to be scared and have my shoes banged on to my head. Sometimes I would automatically find myself waiting there, in the scullery, at the same time.

I would often wake up at the same time, too, sweating with fear after a nightmare. I'd put on the light and wait for dawn.

The days were heavy with nothing to do and I'd try to be helpful to avoid nagging.

I hated every corner of that house. Outside, the black stone, the green paint, the hedge I had to help cut on the side where the drive was, and the pocket-handkerchief lawn at the front. One side of the house was connected to the neighbours', whom we hardly knew. The only time we spoke to Mr and Mrs Brown was when the crates of apples were delivered for the winter, each apple wrapped in tissue paper so as not to contaminate the other. But once, when father was hitting me on my bed, and began to bang my head against the wall, I yelled so loud that Mr Brown came to knock at our front door. I don't know what Daddy told him. I was very much ashamed, after that. I hated being alone in the house with Daddy, but was even more scared to be all alone.

There was only one word that came to my mind as I looked at Aunty Elly. Her head, face, nose, black bun in a net, chest, bottom, tummy and feet were all flat.

From the moment she arrived, Aunty Elly and Mother talked, worked, sat, laughed and went out together. Above all they drank with friends together. They said it helped them. I felt left out. Felt pushed from one place to another, like an unwanted piece of furniture. This sensation made me want to cry whenever I managed to be near Mother. If I did, it made her angry, or cry too.

When she wasn't busy, she'd be rushing off to see lawyers, her navy blue cartwheel hat flopping over her eyes. It accentuated her high cheekbones, throwing soft shadows, as did her long lashes that framed her startling, light-blue eyes. Her dark hair was cut short like a boy's.

Whenever I caught her eye, I'd look imploring. We'd stare at each other, me afraid to blink lest I'd howl. Mother would push out her lips, after a while, and half smiling, half frowning, she'd say, 'Oh! Oh! Olly! Olly! No tears. No tears. Be my brave girl and smile.'

From the day of the funeral to the day of the approaching departure, my stomach behaved like a wild, live thing, never granting me a moment's peace. At night, my knees came up to my chin with spasms, and an iron band and a lead weight seemed to be around and on my chest. In bed I kept having to sit up to try and 'get my breath' like an impossible yawn. The longer I took to 'get it', the more frightened I became of suffocating. Mother now called me hysterical too. I'd grow furious with myself for not being able to get rid of this habit. I'd struggled with it ever since I could remember. When I did manage to fall asleep I'd be plagued with horrible nightmares.

Aunty had been here for a month and today she was to take me away to Basel.

I don't know how I got through that day but by the time we got to the airport I was a nervous wreck. Mummy had had to stay in England to sell the house. I had badly wanted to stay with her and help, but she had refused to allow this.

The feeling that I was suddenly suspended in the sky, with nothing but thin air below to crash into at any moment, made me feel giddy and sick all the way in the plane. I felt deeply ashamed in front of the smart stewardesses and Aunty Elly. I kept looking at the wings, wondering how such heavy long things could not help breaking off. Every part of me was tightened up into one big knot, until we landed. I wondered if my heart would stop, and I would die before ever seeing Mummy again.

The first thing I noticed in Switzerland was that people didn't smile back. Everyone seemed to be in a hurry. They never stood in a queue, but pushed in rudely. The customs officers were bad tempered and, to my surprise, Aunty Elly didn't seem to find this behaviour alarming or unusual. She took on the same snappy tone and looked stern. I'd liked her much better in England when, invited out by our Yorkshire friends, she used to laugh often and looked a lot prettier.

She ordered a taxi. The sight of the Rhine made me long for Mother as I visualised her singing 'Basel on my Rhine' to me with tears in her eyes. She'd cried when she'd talked of the 'Münster', the cathedral which I could now see, in all its beauty, against the twilight sky. It looked safe and welcoming because it was still there, with the red stone towers and huge, diamond-shaped pattern on the roof.

As we drove over the bridge from 'great-Basel' to 'small-Basel', I caught a glimpse of the gold-crowned king-head sculpture on the corner building, poking his long red tongue, which rolled in and out of his mouth, at the 'small Baslers'. The ferry, too, was gliding back and forth on the wire cable strung above the river. All those years, I thought, it had never stopped taking passengers from one bank to the other, while I'd gone to England 'to be a real family'.

Aunty Elly paid the driver and we entered the high-rise apartment building. I nearly fell on the highly polished floor as we entered the lift that took us to the fourth storey.

Everything was spotless.

Uncle Hans, sitting at a table, was reading a newspaper, and I found it strange that he remained seated. Aunt Elly hurried to greet him with a quick peck of a kiss dropped on to his parting.

I went up to shake hands. The room looked like a shop-window display, perfectly tidy, boring and impersonal. Uncle Hans went on reading his paper. I decided he didn't look frightening.

He shouted to his wife, who was already busy in the kitchen, 'I ate at Mother's most days. Three times a week she came round to vacuum clean, tidy and dust. She aired all the beds. It's good to have you back and have real meals cooked again, at home. Mother bought bread and milk and meat, potatoes, onions and a lettuce because I said I'd like a milk-café and a Rösti.'

He returned to the paper, and as he read, he added, 'Go help in the kitchen, child.' He smiled and winked.

After a silent meal, Aunty Elly said, 'You must be tired. I'll show you your room.'

She took me to a bedroom with two beds and said, 'Sometimes you'll be alone here and some nights, when Hans snores, I'll sleep here too. Hurry now. I'll show you where everything is. Come to the bathroom.'

Once the door closed behind her and I was alone, I felt a mixture of relief and despair. I could stop smiling and pretending that everything was all right. But my stomach would not stop cramping and I knew I was in for another night of knees-to-chin spasms. For a short time I got comfort out of lying on the bed like a small parcel. Holding on to my knees made me feel less lonely. After an hour or so of stretching and contracting, I began to feel safe enough to start rolling from one side to the other – my habit of years ago. This way I could get myself exhausted to the point of not thinking, nor feeling. Mother used to call it 'making wum-wum'.

As I began to roll, the bed springs cried out in protest.

I wondered where Mother was now. Tears wet my hair and pillow and I saw and heard Mummy, because I knew she would look at me in that way and say, 'Oh! Oh! Olly! Olly! No tears. No tears. Be my brave girl and smile.'

Before I had boarded the plane I had clung and she'd said, 'Don't make Mummy sad. It's hard enough for Mummy now. Always remember, if you're sad, I'll feel it and be sad too, and if you cry it'll make me cry too. Now you don't want to make me sad, do you? So just be contented and grateful, because things could be a lot worse and we have much to be grateful for.'

I got up and sat on the broad windowsill. As I looked out, I saw that most people must live in flats or apartments here, not houses like in England. I could see people sitting round tables, beneath lamps, doing things together, talking and laughing and sharing. They all had someone who cared.

As I watched, a warm glow spread over me, replacing the sadness by and by. It came from all the lit-up windows. I suddenly knew that there would be other lonely people, somewhere, out there, besides myself and just the fact that there were so many people behind those bright lights shining across the city made me feel better.

I felt relieved because I'd washed my underwear, and hadn't been forced to eat more food than I could manage. (These were my two ever-haunting fears, to be dirty or to be forced to eat. I had never been quite free of them since attending a certain children's home, at Fernsburg in Switzerland.) So there I was, back in the town where I had been born nearly fourteen years before, in 1936. As I couldn't sleep, I went to my bag and got out my diary. I'd always told it my worst worries and my 'nicest memories'. I began to read:

Bradford 1949

I envy Mummy for her drawing and painting talents. She looks so busy, contented and important when she's working on a picture. To watch her makes me feel good about her but I feel so useless. There's nothing I can do well. Tonight they've all gone out. Mummy said Daddy was going to a meeting with Freemasons but that we weren't supposed to know he was there. Frau Dresden went to see another sheep-dog-owner friend and Mummy's at the art club. They won't be long but to me it feels lonely here and the fire's low, not worth stoking up because I've got to go to bed soon. With no fires upstairs the house feels empty. To feel safer and as if I was nearer to Mummy, I usually creep into her room.

I'm in bed now. I was naughty and my heart's still racing. I suppose I wanted to get to know more about Mummy, so I scrounged around a bit. I found an old exercise book in the bottom drawer of her walnut wood chest. I read in it. On every page I found the word 'dirty' more than any other. She finds our house ugly, Bradford dirty, the soot in the air makes her white blouses grey and soils her hands. The fires make her ceilings and walls grubby. The housekeeper's hands are never clean.

It makes me feel sad for Mummy because I know how unhappy she is here, yet there is a lot of beauty and cosiness to be found behind the soot and grime, and she catches this in her pictures and I think she likes to forget everything when she paints, just as I write stories and compositions and my diary because then I too can forget. I wish I'd be good enough to become a writer. I'd also like to be a dancer or actress, but now the best I like doing at school is writing essays and doing gym. I try not to use 'nice' too often and vary my words and look synonims up in the dictionary. It feels good. I'm going to copy out the lovely story my Mummy has written in her own diary. It is the only thing I know about her life before I was born, and I love it. I hope Mummy never finds out I read her exercise book. I'll hurry and smuggle it back as soon as I hear her. She usually comes home in a taxi.

My Mummy's girlhood memories

'We used to live in the country in an old Bernese farmhouse. It's wood-shingle roof came down on all sides, almost to the ground. Only in the front it was cut back, like the fringe on

a forehead, open in ready welcome. To be in the house felt like being protected by a huge mother hen.

'The numerous, toy-like windows, consisting of miniature squares, were decorated by red, pink and white geraniums in window-boxes. I used to love scratching putty away in the glass corners, as we children sat in the niches of the broad window-seats. We'd push up one of the square sliding panels, to pick petals and leaves to press or draw.

'I'll never forget the smell of the sun on the dark, aged wood of the "heat-creaking" house, the "mother-hen"-feeling and the mellodious "bim-bam" of cowbells made me feel contented and secure, gave me company, even in the dark, into sleep.

'Except on nights of thunderstorms! It was flat land and we were taught to have our clothes and shoes ready, always, in case of fire. In case lightning struck.

'Stormy nights had Bernese country folk huddled over the Bible, heavy on the dining-room table, praying and singing hymns in the dim light of the candles. The maids sang Küchenlieder at all times. I dearly love these kitchen songs to this day.

'It was sad that my mother didn't live to see my little girl, my Olly, her only grandchild. To think that she reared eleven children besides myself! And I can hardly remember any of those brothers and sisters except Klaus.

'But I do remember Father. He was from the Appenzell. He was either joking and laughing, or brooding in a corner on the warm oven bench, smoking his quaint Appenzell pipe, upside down, as is the custom to this day. The tobacco was held firmly in place by a silver lid, fastened by a tiny chain. I used to love that pipe. It was the object through which I won his attention and closeness. Whenever I sensed his mood – and I was good at this – I would bring him his leather pouch and pipe and matchbox. (This was, while we still had a home.) He had a belt of shiny black leather with chiselled brass cows, dogs and Appenzell farmers, held firm by the smallest of nails. Similar ornaments adorned our dog's collars and Father's braces which kept up his trousers.

'Everything was decorated! On all doors and beams, on the wood panelling, on cupboards, plate-racks and on all the wood ceilings, were carvings, engravings or painted patterns. In magnificent letters, across the front of our house it said, "God bless the good man".

'Our butter, sweet and white, was pressed into flower moulds. One morning we'd cut off edelweiss to smear on some baked black bread, the next, alpine roses.

'Sometimes Father would play the piccolo or ocarina, or he'd

tap away with tiny hammers on a zither-like instrument, conjuring up gay tunes that made everyone's feet itch to dance. On those nights we were allowed to dress in our national costumes. The farmhands yodelled. I don't know of any better nights in the whole wide world. And they were so simple.

'I was told that when I was born, Father ran through the whole village, telling everyone that "his tulipa" was born. Tulips were his most loved flowers. They grew everywhere and pleased the eye for miles around. Mother arranged some, every day, in the entrance hall. Abundant pastel-shaded shapes bent and stretched gracefully from a hand-painted milk jug on the massive table. The candles, lit on either side, in polished brass holders, threw tulip shadows, as of dancers, on to the wall at night, as we scurried up the stairs and off to bed.

"Ei, du schöne Tulipa" [Oh, you beautiful Tulipa] Father sang and tapped on the zither. It was our flower, our special language. It was my song.

'One day, suddenly, he had gone.

'I missed him painfully, every second at first, like part of myself. Later his memory became like a thought that had slipped my mind. It teased, like a finger on a sore gum, till recaptured, and then it became only a lingering, ever fainter, remembrance. Through gossip I picked up odd whispers of "prison", "debts", "extravagance" and "irresponsibility", but above all I heard the word "alcohol".

I grew more and more frightened as people gave me side glances and whispered "tuberculosis".

'One day, Mother came back from somewhere as she had often done, each time one of her children had disappeared, "Gone to Heaven" as she said. They all went, one after another, much too quickly for me to establish any real relationship with.

'Tuberculosis! On that worst day, Mother wore that black dress and a veil over her face. It was a stranger's face, white, not my Mother's at all. She'd rushed in and hugged Klaus, who was about eight then, and me, aged five. She cried, "Father is no more! This is our house no longer! We must go and find a new home."

'We went to Basel. We had been walking up and down the streets all day in search of work. We were tired and hungry. At last Mother went into a baker's shop. She emerged holding a white paper bag. Our eyes were glued to it as she marched on up the steep hill that lead to the Spalentor, the original tower-gate of the ancient city wall. She stopped in front of a butcher's shop. I will never forget that moment.

'To each of us, Mother then gave a bread bun and said, "Children, I want you to look at those slices of sausages, salami

and ham. As you bite into your bread, keep your eyes fixed on them and you'll be able to taste what you see. Just imagine eating all the meat you want."

'Our mother bit with gusto. With forced mirth she laughed, describing the taste of garlic sausage in a way that I can remember the taste to this day.

'She found work in a small hotel-pension. I remember how quickly she began to look old and frail. I'll never forget her hands. In her free time she painted. Her hands were crippled with arthritis, but nothing could stop her from holding a brush after working hours. As she'd paint, with distorted fingers, there was always that frightening smile, of a woman determined not to recognise defeat. Her flower and ivy pictures were hauntingly beautiful because she set herself motives and mastered all difficulties through daily, constant, disciplined practice.

'Somewhere around that time, I was sent to an orphanage to live. That is the time of my life I shall never speak of or think about. The only thing I can bear to remember is when, feeling like an ill-used servant, I quickly crouched down in the dark corridor and pissed on the macaroni to get revenge for the way I was being treated.

'Mother's health began to fail her. I worked as a dentist's assistant to keep her in hospital. Then I met Marc. The money ran through my fingers. There were too many expenses. Soon Mother was to be placed in the alms-house but Marc was so decent. He prevented that and helped me financially.

'Then she was dying.

'I had long known, but couldn't accept it as a reality. While I was young, I needed desperately to feel alive, especially now that death was knocking on my mother's threshold. Death! Something whose existence I had ignored since Father had so quietly dissolved into thin air, was suddenly visible in the way my mother was wasting away. It was inescapable.

'I'd been at a carnival ball, winning first prize for my daring, crazy costume, when my mother left me forever. She had died alone. Oh, how I despised myself.

'Grief and guilt thrust me into deep depression. I did nothing but quarrel with Marc. I fought my moods. Tried to drown them in alcohol. I chased after life, but my great expectations began to dwindle. My hopes of a life as an artist faded; I would never make it. I had to give up my sculpture and art classes. I gave up all my dreams.

'I remember working as if in a daze. One day, standing next to the dentist's chair, handing him the instruments he required, I must have been miles away in thought. Suddenly a stench

hit my nose. It brought me up with a jolt and I looked down at the wide open mouth, then up at the dentist. An old woman was in the chair. To hold her antiquated false teeth in place and to stop them from rubbing her sore gums, she'd stuffed bits of newspaper underneath her teeth — bit by bit, time after time, until it had all rotted, become infected and stank.

END

I was tired. Through the window, I could see that most of the lights across the city had gone out.

I pushed my diary under the pillow, feeling foolish because I'd dropped a kiss on to the last page. I rolled back and forth lightly and carefully because of the bedsprings and must have fallen asleep.

I dreamed. . . . I feel safe here, in the sandpit behind the house, in England. The sand smells damp and clean. I'm safe because there are no angry voices. Pouring sand into a heap, I pat it flat, then, with my hands, start making patterns, wondering if I could dig a hole so deep that I could crawl through from here to Basel, where Mummy is. I miss her. I'm glad I'm alone, because when I'm not something nasty always happens.

I stand up and let myself fall, flop, into the sand. Grab! Slap! Slap! I throw sand from one hand into the other. Sand flies everywhere. Good smells! Birds sing and chirp because no one worries them. No one pulls their wings or feathers apart to tell them they are horrible, stinking, ugly, ugh, girl-birds. Why is it so bad of me, to be me? I miss my Mummy. I have sand gritty against my teeth and I spit. People who give presents must like people. I hug my bucket and spade close. Mummy gave it to me. I like the sound of my spade hitting the bucket-mountainsides flat. The tunnels underneath keep collapsing! Sand falls away in bits and plops. Rough edges suddenly move as if alive. I get up, cross, and jump everything flat, stamp my feet and inspect what the footprints look like.

Is my Mummy safe? She could get run over by a tram or a car. I squat down to dig a trench and then it happens again! Those horrible feelings that never go away for long, come creeping up my back, up my throat, into my chest and tummy. Every time it happens, I begin to suffocate. Breathing becomes frightening. Air suddenly is a brick wall, refusing to come far enough into me. I gasp, I gulp, lie down flat on my back, lift my bottom, sit up, draw air in and in and in, so it feels like a yawn refusing to be yawned.

And there is that terrible smell! That smell that he punishes me for! It's not in the sand. I kneel down and sniff like a doggy. No! It's me! He and Nanny say, 'Boys don't smell. Girls stink.' Why? If he let Nanny wash me, I could smell of soap and powder and needn't be so sore. But it's forbidden.

I love my bright red overalls that make me feel as good as a boy. Now I'm in my bed. Daddy comes up to the chair beside me and picks up the overalls. Holding their legs wide apart with two fingers at each end, he smells in the middle and pulls a face of disgust. He throws them down, gets my sandal and hits me. I hide under the bedclothes. I feel terrible. He shouts, 'You're a revolting, yuck, phooey, ugh-girl!' The door slams behind him.

I slip out of bed and stand in front of the long, gold-framed mirror. I have to admit, I am very, very small and thin and there's not much colour in my face except for the dark blue eyes and the yellow tufts of hair and fringe.

I say to the girl in the mirror, 'Why are you so disgusting?' I stand and stare and quickly try to smile. For a second I feel better. I don't look as 'revolting' as I had expected. But then I know it's only because I'm wrapped down to my toes in a thick white flannel nightie. Underneath, there is something terrible. Something that is terribly wrong. It's the thing between my legs that spoils everything. It spoils the whole me. He says so. Because of that thing, everybody hates me. That must be the reason why Mummy always leaves me or sometimes sends me away . . . I must give and give and be as good as good can be, to make them forget that I have such a thing on me.

I'm in the sandpit again, hugging my bucket, remembering how I'd been full of waiting and excitement, then heavy and tired when she had finally, really stepped out of the taxi, the last time she came back. There is no feeling like it in the whole wide world. That feeling of being with Mummy. As if I melted into her. As if we were suddenly one whole person. I love her smile and the sound of her voice and the feel of her hands and the look in her eyes. She'd then given me this bucket and spade. It made me feel all warm, with a glow on the inside. Nothing could upset me when she was near me. Why did she go away and make the pain happen again and again? The pain tears apart something inside, much worse than when Daddy hits me. The 'something' is very close to my heart. I can feel it. I'm afraid that it might break and I could die and I'm not allowed to die because I need to be there for Mummy. I must be a good girl because Mummy said if I'm not a good girl one day, and she dies, suddenly, I would regret having been bad on her last day. She cries very much when she has to leave me. Last time, when she left, it happened again. As she drove away in her taxi, the thing on the inside tore a little more, and one day soon, if this doesn't stop, it will tear all the way with the pain. I scrape furrows into the sand and fill my sandals. Mustn't get my bottom wet. But I miss my Mummy and will just sit a little longer. . . .

Suddenly Nanny drags me up by one arm. I didn't notice her coming. She's slapping sand off me.

'There! Come inside! It's time to eat! Why d'you always sit and get damp and scrape the sand inside your sandals? I can hardly get the pants and socks clean. The times I tell you.'

I like her, but am afraid of eating. When Mummy goes away, my tummy presses food out and up my throat as Nanny pushes it down me. Every meal is like a fight. I hate it, three times a day, every day. Hate it as much as what comes after. For the moment Nanny had got the food into me, she seems to want to get it out.

'You will sit on that pot until you produce me your ka-ka.' The cold rim cuts into me. I feel ashamed and uncomfortable. I long for Mummy. And then I can see his eyes coming up the stairs and I cross my arms, and sort of try to fold my legs under me but they hit the pot, so I bend forward to try and look nicer. I hate the smell.

I'm hoisted up like a feather by Nanny. She cleans my botty like a baby's, on top of a table. I'm too big for this! She creams my bottom and face and her hands smell of that horrible smell, now mixed with Nivea. He is always there, then. He stares and is doing something. He says, 'Boys are much nicer. You can't even piddle, standing up!' He does something horrible that gives me cramps in my tummy and I think I'm going to be sick. His eyes grow funny and he goes redder and redder and I want to close my aching legs but he keeps pushing them apart. He never looks at my face. I see a twitching in his cheek that never stops. I want to run and hide but I am very much afraid. He hurts me. Spit dribbles down his chin and little black stubbles point down at me. I dare not move. Suddenly he makes strange noises – like gurgling, spluttering and moaning. He must have hurt himself, because he doubles over and runs to the sink and turns his back on me, and breathes loudly.

Nanny comes back. She had to go away for something. She strokes my bit of sweat-sticky fringe out of my forehead and pulls up my pants. As she lifts me down my legs hurt like after kneeling for a long time. As I hobble away, I feel sore. That thing that is sore is what spoils a little girl. That is what Nanny calls me: 'Little girl, come for a walk.' Or, 'It's time for little girl to go to bed.' I hate the word 'girl'. It makes me see and feel and smell that part of me that is so red and sore and hurts and that he doesn't allow Nanny to bathe. . . .

I'm sitting on my chair, in my room. I close my eyes and flap my arms, which are my wings. I tiptoe out on to the landing and walk up and down, flapping, and suddenly I can fly! I'm a bird and it's all right to be a bird. Even a girl-bird! I fly better and better, but not for long. The wings make a noise and they might hear me and forbid me to fly. So I land on the bannister and jump down and want to try again but suddenly I can't fly any more. I try and I try but I just can't.

Nanny comes and puts me to bed. I sit up to pray as every night, 'Please, God, change me into a boy tonight, please. Let me wake up a boy. Then I'll be a good boy for Daddy, tomorrow. Please God. Goodnight. Amen.'

In my dream I wake up a girl. I know I am dreaming, want to wake up but I can't. I think, if only Mummy would come back. Next to my bed, on the chair, are blue overalls. 'Are they new, Nanny?' I ask.

'What a silly question. You've always had these blue ones.'

'But where are my red ones?' I ask, thinking she's teasing me.

'You never had red ones. You do go on so! What an imagination!'

I ponder this strange information, wondering if I was still asleep. 'But yesterday, in the sandpit, you cleaned the sand off my red ones, on my damp bottom. You said you could hardly get them clean. I had four pairs of red ones.'

'See, there you go again. You weren't in the sandpit yesterday. We didn't have time. We went to see Nanny Smith and you never had any red overalls.'

I run to the drawer. There are three folded pairs of blue ones.

'But Nanny! That was the day before yesterday that we went to see Nanny Smith and of course I had red ones. You put these new ones here! You are a tease!'

I've never seen Nanny get so angry.

She yanks me out of my bedroom and tells me to sit on the lavatory. No potty. I cry-laugh and ask about this new change and am told that I am 'phantasizing'. She says it in German, 'Du phantasierst!' I must have looked bewildered, for she says, 'You always make up things! You always were a good storyteller. Too much imagination!' She continues, 'You've always gone to the lavatory, never a potty, not for a long time.' I grow very frightened at the way she looks at me.

He doesn't come up the stairs that evening, but I'm asked to climb into a bath Nanny's run for me. I don't dare ask any more questions. As she washes me with soapy lather all over, I don't let on how it stings, there. Nanny says, 'This is always the nicest part of the day, isn't it, little girl? We always loved this, every evening, as long as we can remember, didn't we?' She powders and creams my sores, but not on the table like a baby.

Then he is back, but so is Mummy! Suddenly! It's too good to be true and I can't believe it. The three of them talk and look at each other like never before. They even look at me. I think now we are going to be a real, happy family. Then Daddy says, 'There is going to be a war.' Mummy tells me she's taking me back to Basel, that Nanny's going back to Switzerland too, but that Daddy's going to stay in Yorkshire to work in Bradford for the Swiss company. . . .

I don't remember saying goodbye to him. I think, from now on all the pain will stop. I'll be with Mummy forever. . . .

I woke up to find myself rolling and clutching Aunty Elly's duvet, sweating, chanting the words, 'with Mummy, forever, be with Mummy forever. . . .'

I put on the light. I could never remember all the dream but it was often there, haunting, escaping me, just as I wanted to grab and remember. Now, when I woke from it, I felt again as if we had just left England when I was three, just before the War. That's when I'd come to Basel the last time. I sat up because I was afraid to go to sleep again.

Now, Mummy would come to Basel soon and this time everything would be fine. Last time it didn't work because of Hitler. When I was seven or eight, we used to sit in the tearoom called Huguenin. I had seen it today from the taxi. There,

Mummy would sit and talk and laugh with her friends, Aunty Sonja, Aunty Betty and Aunty Maja. I'd sit with them until it was time for me to go to school.

Why do I clearly remember a lady at the table next to ours? She had moved like a filmstar, even crooked her little finger when she drank her tea and had a back that was straight, all by itself, without effort. Her every movement looked as if ready and posing for a photograph. She was all pink skin and sooty lashes and red nails and rustling cream silk and pearls.

For some reason I wanted to cry.

I even remembered how I'd gone to the toilet and when I'd come out of the cubicle, the lady was there, gazing into the same mirror as me. She was very beautiful. She held her head stiffly back, as if posing again. When she'd strode past me, to float out of the room on a cloud of perfume, I had copied the way she walked. I tried to look like her, down my nose, into the mirror and giggled. I yearned for Mummy and for the rare moments when she'd say, 'Olivia, you have such a delightful sense of humour.' I'd been glad I'd been good that day. Not like the time I had been made to stand in a corner for the whole restaurant to see, because I hadn't eaten my spinach.

On the way back to Mother's table I had gone to my favourite waiter with the side whiskers and kind eyes, to ask if I could look at the children's books. He had given them to me, out of the drawer behind the counter where all the cakes were. He had waddled like a duck because he had very flat feet. I loved to watch him.

Mummy had made a fuss, as always, and excused me for bothering him. I'd looked at the books to hide my blushing face.

When it was time for me to go to school, I would kiss Mummy and the aunties and walk down the wide, curved, carpeted stairs to the exit. I used to feel quite grown-up, alone in the streets of Basel. Once, in the tram, I had tried to talk to an old woman next to me because she looked sad. She had given me a 'be quiet' look and turned away.

I used to jump down from the tram, satchel rattling, and hop on one leg across to the pavement, then I'd hop on the other leg to be fair to both legs. All the way to school I wasn't allowed to stand on a crack in the pavement. It would bring on lots of bad things if I did. I was happy till I reached the huge red stone building with the tower and clock. It always seemed to squash me, so that I could hardly walk up the grey cement stairs which had bits chipped off. My hand became sweaty on the cold iron railing, I hated the smell of pencil lead, leather, floor-polish and disinfectant soap. It always took courage to walk into my classroom. . . .

At Gotthelf school, when I was nine, Yvette was the prettiest girl in my class, and I wanted to be her only friend. But she wanted many friends. She already had parents and a brother and they had games and did fun things together. Even though Mummy had painted flowers and hearts, red and blue and green, on to my bed and wardrobe, it didn't make me feel less lonely. She often went out. I didn't mind, as long as I could live with her. By now I couldn't remember my father. We didn't have any photographs. Food was rationed. There was much talk about the war and I only thought of him when we prayed at night. 'Please, God, don't let a bomb fall on Daddy's head in England.' But then, being still in Bradford, he was much further away from Hitler.

Everybody hated Hitler. On our return to Switzerland, Hitler was the reason Mummy had first sent me away to live with Nanny's parents in Zürich. We lived too near the German border. We were on the border of France, too, because our teacher called Basel the 'three lands' corner'. We all knew that if Hitler crossed the frontiers, he would kill us all or treat us like Jews, who were gassed alive, even the children. I often couldn't go to sleep at night for fear of him. In my mind I frequently wrote long letters to Hitler.

Dear Mr Hitler,
Please don't catch and kill the Jews. Please don't fight with the whole world. Germany is so big and beautiful. It is all yours, so why can't you be contented with your country? The Swiss are satisfied with Switzerland and it is much smaller. Why shouldn't every country just have its own country and be contented? You see, Jews are just people. Just humans like you and me. With the same feelings. Didn't your mother teach you to be kind and loving? Or didn't you get enough love? I'll love you and help you to tell people that this World belongs to everybody and everybody has a right to be happy in it. What does your mother have to say about all the dreadful things

you do? And your conscience? What if there *is* a God? Has she seen photographs of your concentration camps? How can you live and sleep when mothers and fathers and children get separated from each other, lose each other, suffering agonies because they don't know if they are all still alive? Please, Mr Hitler, stop all this. At school we're just learning about Jesus who was so kind and loving, although they killed him, too. Couldn't you read about him? It's a very good book called the Bible. I'm sure, deep down, you are very nice because they say you love Alsaitian dogs and Beethoven and a lady called Eva Braun. Imagine if someone killed her or your mother or dog? You wouldn't like that, would you? I like dogs too, and Beethoven, although Mozart better, but I'm sad he lost his hearing. My Mummy did too, in one ear, and she gets very tired when people talk a lot. Beethoven must have been sad not to even hear his own music again, after composing it. Mozart sounds happier, although his wife had T.B. like my grandfather and made many debts like him too. Maybe his music would cheer you up more so that you don't do these nasty, cruel things. I'm sure if you find someone to really love you, you will see what I mean. Heidi and Yvette, who are my friends, send their love, too, because we are sure you must be sad or sick or don't know what's going on. All our love and please take this seriously and think about it.

Love, Olivia.

I'd feel better after doing this sort of thing, while in the room next door I could hear Mummy talking about Hitler, in a hushed, frightened voice. It all used to send prickly feelings down my spine and my eyes would water. So while I'd be composing these letters to Hitler, I'd be throwing myself back and forth, in my wum-wum fashion, till I fell asleep.

I couldn't 'stay with Mummy forever' — never could stay long at all, really. So after we left England, when I was nearly four, there was more goodbye-pain and crying. I had to go in a train with Nanny. Nanny told me her father was an engine-driver and her mother baked beautiful cakes and that she, Nanny, had to go and work for another family. I remember how I thought the floor of the train was going to crash through and I'd fall under the big wheels I could hear racing beneath us.

I was allowed to call them Gross-mamma and Gross-papa.

They were lovely. In their warm wooden chalet, they tucked me up under a huge duvet in the little 'trench' between them, in the middle of their high, giant twin beds. I rocked back and forth as I usually did, and held on tight to the duvet, but I was less afraid there because they would be beside me, later.

Nanny was gone in the morning, but Gross-mamma sat me on the table in the kitchen and gave me some dough to make a cake of my own. Later, taking me shopping, she talked to me as to a real person. She really looked at me when she talked. Told all the neighbours about her daughter being my nanny in England, and they all smiled at me properly and said I could come and play with their children. In the shops the shopkeepers gave me a reel of sausage at the butcher's, a bun at the baker's and an apple at the grocer's. I had never been so spoilt and couldn't thank them enough. Gross-mamma said it was enough to say thank you once.

On the way home, past the 'Casärne' where young soldiers did their military training and became 'men', we came to the red and white railway crossing with the barrier just coming down to the clanging of a bell. Gross-papa's train was due and she gave me a white hanky. I felt important because I knew him, and I waved like mad. I caught sight of his huge moustache and a twinkling eye, before he was gone with thunder. The speed, power and roar of the engine made my insides feel like a drum being thumped. Beaming at each other, Gross-mamma and I walked home hand in hand. There, everything smelled of baking and we sat down and ate what we'd made earlier, then went out to collect beans and berries from the garden, which was another real miracle.

Kurtli came to play and we made puddles in a sandpit and caught frogs with our buckets and put them in the lakes we had made. We had such a lot of fun, till he stood at the side and opened his trousers and pulled out something, splashing a streak of yellow water on to the earth. As I looked, I felt a horrible feeling climb and clutch all over me and I couldn't breathe and choked and ran into the kitchen, crying and shivering.

I liked washing days, when the village was in an uproar and the houses and countryside smelled of soapsuds and fresh 'wetness'. Gross-mamma and the washerwoman stirred the piles of washing in a giant's copper with wooden spoons as big as trees. At night we all went to bed at the same time, pushing noses into clean, sun-dried sheets and pillows.

I waited, every evening, for Gross-papa to come. When he returned I'd watch his every move, which never changed. He'd walk in, place his cracked leather, sausage-shaped bag behind the door and stride over to the stone sink to lather his hands twice. He would then come over to the table to carefully unfold his clean white hanky. Back at the sink, he used to turn on the tap with the red rubber tube attached and bend down. With one finger and thumb he would close a nostril, snorting the one, then the other clean of snot and soot. Only then would he use his hanky.

He used to pat me on the head before he sat down, always laughing. Then Gross-mamma would bring milk coffee in his Swiss 'Gungele', a moon-cup with flat ears, so big that he lifted it by placing both his hands underneath. He would slurp blissfully and say, 'Ahhh!' while she handed him his round wooden board with bread and cheese. He used to slice neat strips towards his thumb, and then dip the bread into the coffee. Gross-mamma would sit down and watch him as if it gave her great pleasure and they would look into each other's eyes. It made me feel warm and good. Everything they did seemed important. And neither he nor she were ever in a hurry. The work they did seemed fun and they treated it as if it was a privilege to do. And there was always time to laugh and play.

Just before this life came to a sudden end, like good things always did, Gross-papa woke us at four one morning. He wanted to show me, his 'new country-girl', her first sunrise. We all dressed, yawning, before walking out into the chilly moon-freshness to get a train. Gross-papa, not driving it for once, didn't have to buy a ticket. He knew all the people. The trees on the side of Mount Etzel stood as if they were all his silent friends. The stillness made me feel shivery in a good way. A scramble here and there told us of hidden animal life. We hardly talked and it felt grown up to be part of the silence. After a long walk Gross-papa hoisted me up onto his shoulders and I loved him for carrying me so I didn't say how uncomfortable it grew, after a while. But then I forgot because everything was suddenly bathed in pink and gold and purple and pale blue and silver, and I couldn't believe my eyes. A red ball of blood rose out of nowhere and lit up the night into day, lighting up my whole inside too.

I became aware of them both watching me, smiling at each

other and I knew that I was not so alone. We were all together in this joy, sharing the miracle of a new morning. Every day was a present to be grateful for. 'Who makes all this happen and who makes the things that can make it happen?' I whispered, the question pushing harder than the need for silence.

'God in heaven, Olivia, God. We must never forget how much we have to say thank you for. And here you can say it, over and over again.' I smiled at Gross-mama and we all held hands and sang together, 'Thank you, liebe Gott'. We sang it in a canon, all the way down hill, like a march melody, up and down the scales.

That night I went to bed early and could stop rolling and didn't even have to hold on to the duvet. I had never been so happy in all my life. I heard Gross-papa roaring past the bottom of the garden in one of the trains and I knew that everybody was safe.

The next day Nanny came and I cried, although I was now going back to Mummy. Gross-mama sat me on her lap and I looked into her lovely face. Her blue eyes were set deeper than I'd ever seen and her hair was silvery white. 'The place in the middle of our beds will always be there for you and you are our only grandchild,' she said. . . .

I often dreamed about them too, and woke up crying because I'd never seen them again and knew that now they were both dead.

I got up to sit on the windowsill. All the windows for miles around were dark now. I must be the only person awake in the whole of Basel, I thought, and wondered if Mummy, in Bradford, was asleep and if she'd managed to sell the house.

I shut out all memories of the attic room, where apples were stored for winter, where he made me. . . . No! Forbidden!

What happened next, after Gross-mamma and Papa? Well, not so bad, but leading up to bad memories. The first were good. Mummy loved Andreas, who was a doctor. His wife said she'd let him go, but posed a condition. They were not to see each other for a year. Mummy and I went therefore to live in the Italian part of Switzerland. I'd seen it in calendars many times. Everybody loved it. But to live there! And with Mummy!

It was a nice life in a hotel and a lady looked after me at night. One night Mummy was locked out and she developed meningitis and had to have everything removed behind one ear. She only hears in one – and I always forget which one. Another night I felt the need to tell her that I felt so ashamed because I didn't have what boys had, in front. I thought she could help me because I thought about it always, and felt something was missing on me, wrong with me. But she just laughed. Why did I feel so ashamed because I was a girl? Hated myself! Something is missing and wrong.

Then we came to move into a new apartment on the fourth floor of a block in Basel. It had glass doors and a balcony and was grand. Mummy's furniture had names like Biedermeier and Chippendale and there were glass cases and knick-knacks and gold-framed mirrors. But though Mummy said that, after the war, Daddy would give her a divorce, Andreas's wife wouldn't.

I went to the red stone school where I had first met Yvette.

I remember day-dreaming about 'my grandparents in Zürich' in class because they made me feel safe. One day Mr Meier, my teacher, shouted, 'Olivia!' I jumped, and he said, 'Have you heard one single thing I've said, in this classroom, this afternoon?'

I said, 'No,' and the children shrieked with laughter. He'd asked something about a train going at a speed of 100 km an hour from Basel to Zürich and if the two cities were 100 km apart, how long would the train take? I remember how I smiled and said, 'The train from Basel to Zürich takes one-and-a-half hours. I know because my Gross-papa is an engine driver and he lives there and I've been on the train.'

He'd shouted that the train in the book didn't stop and drove straight there at a speed of 100 km an hour and would I please concentrate on the train in the book and not talk about a gross-papa nobody was interested in.

That had made me cry. How could anyone not be interested in him, and anyway, he knew more about trains than the silly book. They could never understand me and I could never understand the things everyone else seemed to understand.

Yvette had whispered, 'One hour,' and I repeated it and loved her passionately.

'Thank God for that!' Mr Meier had said. 'And in future spare us the stories of your relatives.'

'She hasn't got any real relatives, really. She told me so,' Yvette whispered again, so loudly that all the children and the teacher heard. I hated her. Hated being different. Everybody had relations and family and were never so alone. They were cruel and had no right to be, because they had much more fun and things.

After school Mr Meier kept me in and I had to walk home alone. I forgot about not standing on cracks and ran up the four wooden flights of stairs, glad to be home.

Mummy shouted from the phone, 'I'll be with you in a minute. Got a bone to pick with you!'

My tummy tied its usual knot in my middle. I walked into my bedroom and stood and stared. All my drawers were pulled out and clothes, toys and books were one big pile in my room. Mummy was laughing on the phone. I quickly began to fold and rearrange my things back where they belonged.

'For goodness sake. Take your satchel and coat off. All day I work and clean and tidy and everything that you don't do, I have to do, too. From now on, I always want your room tidy, and no messy drawers!'

She was watching me take off my coat and as I put it down, to immediately go on with my tidying, she jumped and said, 'No! See! Put things where they belong! Instantly! Then they don't clutter up.'

I went to hang up my coat. My room took forever and I knew I had lots of homework and I was thirsty.

Mummy came in later with biscuits and raspberry cordial. I sat down, watching her having to tidy the rest away. I felt guilty, specially as she rearranged nearly everything I'd done.

'Tonight you must write that thank-you letter to Nanny for the parcel she sent you.'

'I've got lots of homework.'

'You've got all evening. I'm going out. Aunty will help you. Now, first write the letter.'

Wondering which aunty was going to pop out of the hat, like a rabbit at a magician's, I nibbled the end of my pencil. I hated writing letters because Mummy was so strict. I never knew what to say after, 'How are you. I am well. Thank you for the lovely present.' I made up some more and went to show it. She told me what I already knew – that I was slipshod and scribbled and made stupid mistakes and had to copy it out again. After I'd copied the big page for the fifth time, all smeared with tears, Mummy said she had to talk to me seriously.

'Sit down opposite me, Olivia. I've got to go out soon, but I must tell you that Mr Meier rang up.' (Another knot in my stomach.)

'Your teacher says you daydream and can't concentrate and can't think logically.' (I'm an idiot! I knew it.) 'He has also noticed that your tic has gotten worse.' (They tell me I squeeze my eyes closed in a frenzy, for seconds, every so often and then open my mouth, wide, as if to help to get my eyes open again.)

Mummy takes my hands and scolds me for the bitten nails. 'Honestly, dearling, they're raw and bleeding. Gnawed down to the roots. How can you be such a cannibal with yourself?' She lets go and I look at her, wishing I could sit on her lap, wishing she'd touch me.

'The doctor says you are a very nervous child and need to be with other children, so he has suggested a good home for you — Fernsburg, where they teach school so you won't fall behind. I'm taking you tomorrow. It will be very good for you, and don't make Mummy sad by crying. I'm just as sad as you are.'

I went to my room with the red hearts and forget-me-nots, to do my homework. On my way, I went to Mummy's bed to get Michael, the new puppy Mummy had been given by Andreas a short while ago, but Mummy shouted. 'Leave Michael on my bed.' He was usually either there or on Mummy's lap. Why did I have to go away but he could stay?

In the last home, I mused, fighting back tears, I'd learnt to ski and make paper dolls. I never stopped making clothes for them. As long as I was making things, I was all right. No one had forced me to eat more than I could, like at my godmothers' or other aunties or families I'd stayed with. The people at the last home had been kind. Only the first night, after I raced up stone stairs to the phone and fell and grazed both shins, I had been sad, because Mummy had sobbed when she heard me crying. . . .

'I'm going out now. Come and say good evening to Aunty Grabeli.' Mummy looked lovely.

This aunty was a gentle, nice old lady, I liked. She always read to me with a shaky voice in sad parts, stopping to wipe away a tear at times. This time she read about war-refugee children who had lost their parents and were going to be adopted in another country. It comforted me to hear of children who had a much worse life than I, and they were younger too. I was nine.

Aunty Grabeli tucked me in and later came to ask if I didn't get a headache from rolling so hard and so long. Once I woke up that night, yelling I'd lost my red overalls in the sandpit and was a bird and didn't need trousers any more. I could remember digging in the sand, but never much more of the dream that came again and again.

When I woke up the next morning, I was rolling and clutching the duvet, sweating and chanting words. I remember looking round my newly tidied room and seeing my open-mouthed suitcase on the floor, like a frightening crocodile with gaping jaws. It had jolted my memory. It was the day I was to go to the new children's home, at Fernsburg.

The windowsill at Aunty Elly's was broad and made of cream-coloured marble. My bottom was freezing. I climbed back into bed and pushed my pillow up against the wall. I was still wide awake. Here I was, back in Basel, trying to remember nice memories and they were all mixed up with sad ones. But Mummy always said it was me. I had a negative, selfish attitude and took myself too seriously.

I'd written a story about my stay at Fernsburg, when I was younger and I turned to it now.

MY MOST HATED PLACE

I knew crying wouldn't help.

Mummy was having a cup of coffee and smoking a cigarette. It was one of those days called 'tropisch' in Basel, sticky and hot. As I sat on the corner bench and looked Mummy in the eyes, my chin began to wobble as she said, 'Don't tyrannise me, Olivia. Don't. It's just as hard for me.' I hated it when she said this. It made me feel so helpless.

After the train, it was a hard walk up a mountainside. Mummy was too elegant and looked angry and uncomfortable. I couldn't catch her eye, so tried to hold her hand but the narrow path forced me to let go. All I could think of was that if Hitler came she could die, all alone, in our apartment and I wouldn't be able to help, wouldn't know and would have no one in the whole wide world. Suddenly she went all soft and dear and gathered me to her, in front of a cement building. 'I have problems to sort out. It has to be and it's the best for you, believe me, dearling.'

A tall woman in black stockings came out to greet us. Her hand felt dry and rough. They talked, walking away from me, looking in my direction every now and then.

The woman said her name was Miss Hand and she pointed to a bench, in the distance, at the other side of a small wood and said, 'You may accompany your mother to that bench, if you promise to come straight back. It's called the "tear bench".' I wondered what they found to laugh about.

So we stood by the bench, on a small hill, in the centre of a green meadow dotted with bright yellow buttercups and dandelions. For one awful moment I thought I was going to fill my pants – I'd had a stomachache all day. For one long moment we clung together, painfully. The next, Mummy almost brutally pulled herself free and ran down the mountain.

I followed her for as long as I could, with my eyes thinking of my bed with the flowers and hearts she had painted for me, thinking of the new puppy she'd just got, that was allowed to stay. I saw butterflies and ants and thought they were all luckier than me.

It took courage to enter the building. I found everybody in a dining room. Boys and girls, silent at many tables, stared. Miss Hand pointed to a chair as she walked round with a terrine of soup.

I stammered, 'Thank you,' but my plate was filled to the brim and didn't seem to get emptier, as hard as I tried. Miss Hand then came with cabbage, potatoes and meat and sloshed it all into my soup. I spluttered on through tears and shame. I suddenly remembered that Mummy often said I took myself too seriously. She had said, 'Keep a sense of humour.' Maybe this was a sort of test or a joke? Hopefully I looked around, but there wasn't a joke in sight for miles, because now Miss Hand was pouring plum and applesauce with custard over my plate. Everyone was staring at me.

All the children who had eaten marched in two files out of the room.

Four of us sat, scattered, then three, two, and, for a very long time, I sat alone. I was told that children who didn't eat up were in disgrace and had to sit by their beds till suppertime. But then, again, I couldn't eat. My throat and tummy were closed. I was told I'd have to eat my macaroni cheese for breakfast the next morning.

We all had to put on white linen uniform nighties and stand in two rows. I didn't know what for and went quickly to obey. To my absolute horror, I saw that the children were holding up their underpants for inspection. I was told to go and get mine.

How their eyes looked! They made me turn mine inside out and hold them up. The teachers were coming down the lines, searching for tiniest marks, spots or stains. One child was told it had 'badly soiled its underwear' and had to drag its heavy mattress to the cellar. She was not allowed to take covers, and was told, 'No drinks all tomorrow and you are to talk to no one.'

Standing at the end of the queue, I was shaking with fright. I'd had an accident, because of my tummyache all day making me have diarrhoea, but worst of all, I'd done a dreadful thing and it was going to be found out any minute, in front of all these new faces! Not having been able to swallow all the tough meat and cabbage, I'd pushed a huge lump up my bloomers, from time to time, when nobody was looking. Now my underpants were all stained, green-brown-stringy-slimey!

Nearer and nearer they came. I was going to be sick any minute.

Miss Hand pulled me out of the line, by my ear. 'What have we here? Is this how you treat food! Ja, ja, you are an only child, eh? An evil, spoilt, only child! Go to my room upstairs and wait.'

In great fright, I scurried up some wooden stairs, just standing at the top, not knowing where to go, punishment ahead. 'Mummy!'

She came, after a long time, steps silent as a cat's stalking it's prey. She made me stand in a corner, behind a door, for one hour.

Shaking and icy cold, I climbed into one of the iron beds standing in rows. I wondered what it was like in the concentration camps people were talking about.

A cock shrilly 'kikerikied' me out of sleep. I saw sixteen beds. I had to race into the grey corridor, in search of a toilet.

I sat, letting out pent-up spasms, making noises I hoped desperately no one would hear. I looked at my dangling toes and saw my mother's feet, mine smaller but just the same, the left one slightly inward-pointing when we sat or walked. What was she doing now? I hoped she wouldn't be too sad and lonely without me.

No toilet paper! Why did these unexpected things happen? I found some in the cubicle next door, stayed there and sat on the lid. The rising sun began to paint the walls of the ugly place into pink prettiness. For a few minutes a great peace and new strength came over me. I wished time would stand still, to let me hide and rest, here forever.

Back in the dormitory, I looked round at all the sleeping children and wondered where all their mothers were. All the laps and arms, I suddenly felt the need for closeness. I longed for Mummy.

In the far corner, under a picture of a sweet, lolly-coloured Jesus, a small girl began to sniffle. I noticed that her face looked sad. She moved like an old person who had given up all hope. I watched her pull apart her bedding and carry her sheets across the room, stumbling. I got up to help.

She looked even more frightened and said, 'I'm not allowed to talk to anyone because I wet my bed.'

Through the window above my head I saw her go up to a wooden trough, pushing her heavy bundle into cold water as well as she could. Later I heard the children chant, 'Smelly Nelly with the red paws!'

This was the worst place I had ever been to.

For breakfast we had a mug of milk with thick skin on top which we had to swallow, and a piece of brown bread. Only the teachers had butter and jam, because there was a war on. They must have forgotten my macaroni, but at every midday and evening meal I sat chewing and crying for hours in front of a plate of gooey, messy food.

Miss Hand made beautiful flower costumes for us out of crêpe paper. She made up musicals that were famous in all the schools and children's homes in Switzerland, and I was a little snowdrop. Some boys were beetles and insects. Everybody said how gifted, patient and musical she was and *so* wonderful with the children. We all looked up to her.

Why all the other children could eat was a puzzle to me and made me feel the weakest, most miserable failure. Always different. All the other children could run, barefoot, across newly cut stubble of cornfields. My feet hurt and bled and I was forever last, trying to catch up without crying.

One day a big boy, with red hair, who was proud he was strong, offered to take me on his back across such a field, on an outing. As he ran, he panted, 'I know how to make people.'

'Nobody but God knows that!' I answered.

'*I* know,' he insisted stubbornly. Our argument was overheard and we both were summoned to Miss Hand's room that night. She asked us something about 'an indecent conversation'. We didn't understand why she said we had been wicked. I felt terrified because I seemed to be such a bad person who could not eat or sleep or wear underpants or even talk without doing something sinful and wrong.

The next day was Sunday. We all had to dress in our best. I was just about to bite into my piece of bread when Miss Hand ordered silence. She called out, 'Olivia and Jacob, come here!' I couldn't understand nor believe it when she said, 'Olivia and

Jacob have used their mouths to speak of filthy things! For this they have to be punished.'

I had only talked to the big boy about God. What had I done and what were they going to do to me now? I looked around, but there was no way out.

She was still talking, 'So you two will not repeat to us the obscene conversation you had yesterday, ja, ja . . .?' She was sticking an enormous cross of sticky band-aid tape over the boy's mouth. Another teacher came to hold my head and Miss Hand came to stick one on me. We had to go to church with the sticky cross over our mouths.

I didn't have to eat the sloshy mess that day. The next day, they told us that the war was over.

Hitler hadn't won! I was soon to go back home. . . .

Three in the morning! I hadn't read those parts of my diary for ages. I couldn't stop. . . .

Hitler didn't come, nor were we treated like the Jews but Father came.

As I arrived home from school one day, I could hear Mummy crying and laughing on the phone. She was telling somebody that my father had come from England to take us back to live with him in Bradford. She put the phone down and looked at me.

She dressed me in my light-blue coat with the white fur collar and cap, and sent me down to meet him, in front of the apartment house.

'But, I don't know him.'

Mummy didn't react. She seemed more upset than joyful.

I stood and watched people rushing past, till I saw one man, limping, coming slowly towards me. I felt wobbly because I hoped this man wasn't him.

He had a dark blue beret on his head, as if to hide a bald patch. He wore gold-rimmed spectacles like Mr Meier, on a thin nose in a bony face. The deep lines from his nose to the corners of his lipless mouth looked severe. He was tall and lean, toppling to the left at every step, dragging one leg a little. I felt sorry about that. I found out later that his sneer was his smile. It often turned into anger, with no warning.

As he got nearer, and looked down, I could see a muscle jumping all the time in his left cheek. How had such a beautiful woman as my mother been able to marry such a strange-looking man?

Summoning all my courage, I kept on looking up at him and,

smiling as brightly as I could, I said, 'Excuse me, Sir, are you my father?'

He answered, 'No. I'm your daddy!'

I could hardly bear to read on, but I had to. I wondered if things had turned out like they had because I hoped that he wasn't my father, when I saw him? I wondered whether, at that first meeting, if I'd had some really loving thoughts, as if by magic, everything would have been different? Poor Daddy. Dead now.

I felt like cold stone inside. Frozen. I continued to read.

ANOTHER NEW HOME AND A NEW COUNTRY AND A FATHER!

All my memories seem to blur after that. All the aunties and Mummy's friends and Andreas seemed as upset as she was. There was much crying and confusion and talk of 'mines in the sea', what to do with Michael the puppy (who was now a big dog), what to take of the furniture, and that it was a terrible shame the doctor could still not get a divorce.

Suddenly we were on a night-train to Paris and next on our way to the boat to Dover. Mummy said everybody got sick on boats, so I felt instantly sick the second I saw it. I was also scared stiff it would blow up any minute. Somewhere, someone was selling bananas. No one had eaten any for years and everyone wanted to buy some. We were all crowded into a room with rows of bunks reaching from the floor to the ceiling. Women and children were fighting to get such a bunk. Mummy got one underneath me. I felt sick. Daddy stayed on deck. Later, once we were on our way, everyone vomited bananas from one bunk down to the next! Sour banana-vomit-smell was the air we breathed, and every time we did, we were even more sick. I asked Mummy if I could please die, and she said one didn't, but everyone who was seasick thought they might, and that this was a proper sign of real seasickness and therefore I was experiencing the real thing. I nearly felt proud!

In Dover the earth wouldn't stop rocking like the sea. We went to a hotel and I had to sleep with Daddy in a huge bed. I didn't know why, but the sound of the foghorn scared me and the bright beam of the lighthouse never stopped circling our bedroom for long and it was impossible to sleep. I didn't know Daddy.

We took the train to Bradford. Daddy sounded very fond of it when he called it 'mucky old Bradford', but it really was a sooty, black, grimy town and Mummy looked shocked.

There was a German housekeeper, Frau Dresden, to meet us. She seemed pleased to see Daddy, gave me a box of sweets and chewing-gum, but ignored Mummy. We drove, in a taxi, through streets of black stone houses with windowframes and doors painted in shiny greens, reds, blues and whites.

I couldn't understand a word anybody said in English, like the porter and the taxi-driver, but they seemed to smile more than the Swiss did.

We drove past a long hospital and then up the steep hill in Cranbourne Road which was lined on both sides with the same semi-detached houses, everyone's alike out of that same black stone, excepting for the colours on their doors and windows. One of them, number eight, was ours. It was three storeys high and had a gable, a drive and a garage, painted green.

Soon I was sent to Dairy Hill School, up the hill. On the third day boys and girls came to me and said, 'Good morning, guten morgen. It means fuck, you say fuck to the teacher. It means guten Morgen, good morning.' I hadn't a clue what it was all about, but as they seemed so pleased and had learned a bit of German, I stood up and proudly said 'Fuck' to the teacher, who got angry with me, but then with the children. I learned quickly and it was a happy time. They shared their words, Yorkshire dialect, lunch, games, fights and lice with me. Public school treated me as an equal. Now I was tired, I didn't want to think about the next school.

Again, I pushed the diary under my pillow and snuggled down into my bed. What a good thing Aunty Elly was sleeping in the other room with Uncle. I could sleep now. A whole new life lay in front of me and I was going to make 'only good memories'. From now on it would be Mummy and me – and she had promised to bring Glenny, my dog.

In the morning Aunty came to wake me, at eleven, with the good news that 'Your mother is coming to Basel in a week! Andreas just phoned.'

'I'll have my mummy and my dog.'

'Yes. Get up now and we'll have a lovely breakfast together.' Aunty Elly was suddenly the loveliest, best-looking, dearest aunty anybody had ever had in Basel!

Chapter Five

Andreas picked us up and we went out to celebrate. We drove past the Schutzenmatt park where, when I was little, I used to drink goat's milk, pretending I loved it to please Mummy, then past the house where we'd lived in the apartment on the top floor.

'Our old apartment, Andreas. Do you remember the zebra you gave me? I still have it.' He smiled and nodded as he parked the car in front of the Schützen-haus, one of the finest restaurants.

Aunty Elly and Uncle Hans enjoyed their food and wine. They ate all the time Andreas talked. And how he talked – of Mummy and of the long years of suffering, now finally coming to an end, and how he had left his wife and children, how for twelve years they had longed for each other, how his wife wouldn't give him a divorce and made him pay through the nose, but how nothing mattered now, nothing stood between them, for at last his beloved Ida was free and coming home.

I knew how he felt, because I was always longing and yearning for her. As I ate my *Bratwurst* and *Rösti*, my favourite meal, all I could think of was that Mummy, my Mummy, would soon be close – close to me with my dog, Glenny. The many painful goodbyes were over. When she used to have to leave me in Bradford with Father and Frau Dresden, to go to Basel and to Andreas, so often I'd waited for her return with an intensity of expectations so exhausting that there was no joy left to show when she truly and finally arrived. Next week would be different! I could hardly eat. From now on it would be a new, wonderful life together.

The restaurant was full of elegant people, visibly and audibly enjoying food, wine and each other's company. Andreas was saying how much bother and agony my mother had to face all alone. The house had been hard to sell and the will had revealed that Frau Dresden was left in charge of the car plus a large sum of money.

'I wonder what there was between Marc and that woman!' Andreas was saying. I nearly choked on my sausage. These were the moments when I had to be quick in trying to hold shut the shutters on my memories, but it grew more and more difficult every time. I couldn't swallow. The strain and effort of trying not to remember Father was becoming unbearable. I concentrated on a fly on the ceiling. Keeping my eyes glued to it, I thought, it has six legs, two wings. It can fly. I was that fly, when Father did it to me. I'm that fly now. Flies don't feel, don't think, don't know, don't smell things, otherwise they couldn't sit on shit. . . .

'What on earth are you staring at? Olivia! Behave! Eat nicely! What are you blowing your cheeks up for, with all that food, like chewing-gum? The child is crazy! Teenagers! I ask you? I hope your mother finds you on your best behaviour.'

They continued to talk and forgot about me.

I picked a huge pimple on my chin. I absolutely didn't want it there when Mummy arrived. I wondered if I could squeeze it while they talked. I dabbed at the blood with my serviette – stealthily, seeing the many tiny red spots on the white cloth.

'Your mother was always telling you not to pick your spots. Stop it! No wonder they spread. Soon you'll look like a *Streussel-kuchen*. One would think you'd like to look your best.'

As they went on talking, I tried hard not to bite my fingernails. There wasn't much left to bite.

'Her unselfconsciousness and complete lack of pose and mannerisms gives her a natural genuineness, a sort of grace I have never seen in a woman.' They all agreed with Andreas that my mother was uniquely fascinating. (For a moment I'd hoped they were talking about me.)

In the centre of the table a delicate fuchsia hung like a scarlet lantern. I made it swing by moving the high, slender, silver vase, and the flower glowed like a flame as it caught the candlelight. The vase suddenly tripped, toppled and fell, spilling and splashing the table and Aunty. She let out a yelp like a puppy. Fuss and commotion! A waitress came to dab at the water between the plates and dishes, while I sat crimson under the glare of Aunty Elly and hundreds – thousands – of people.

'I'll speak to you later.' Stonily she flung this at me.

As I furtively looked up and over at the next table, I saw a girl of my age. As our eyes met, a current of wordless, sympathetic understanding flowed between us. I smiled, and suddenly a great wave of joy broke over my head. I suddenly remembered rolling in the heather on my Yorkshire moors in the sunshine, just laughing with my dog, Glen, warming my cold body, after memories had haunted me all day at school, after a bad night with my father. There again! The shutters wouldn't stay closed. Opening for nice flashbacks, they tricked me into nasty ones. I looked back to the girl. She was just leaving. Soon we left too.

As the adults took an evening stroll through the park, I looked over at the house we'd once lived in. It was funny, but one morning a child, somewhere down here on this very road, had called, 'Mummy!' It was early Sunday morning and my mother had answered in a most annoyed manner at having been woken up, 'What?'

'Mummy!' the child had yelled again. 'It's too early,' my mother complained.

'Mummy!' Again! I remember cringing in bed, but with delight at the audacity of anyone daring to do something against my mother's strict rules. Finally she had found out and laughed with me. Only from 10 o'clock onwards did I dare to go and snuggle up with her on Sundays. I'd take a long piece of string with a key on and I'd knot and unknot this string for hours.

Once I'd had a wonderful birthday party in that house, inviting girls from school, including Yvette. I had adored Yvette! On the first day of school I'd whispered to Mummy that I'd like to stand in row with the beautiful little black-haired, black-eyed girl. She had at the same moment asked her mother if she could stand in line with the little blonde, blue-eyed girl. From then on we'd been inseparable, although we often fought one day and made up the next. We had never lost contact over all these years. I decided to ring her soon. Peter, too. Yvette and Peter had written to me all the time I was in England. He was at boarding school and Yvette on holiday now.

I'd met Peter at the ballet classes Mummy used to take me to, once a week. (Strangely, I suddenly remembered how, as I used to put on my ballet tights, I though there was something wrong with me because I was flat at the front, below, and wasn't a boy. I wonder why?) I had been chosen to dance at a parent's evening with other girls and had to dance a Mozart minuet. As I'd finished and bowed to the applause, a small boy rushed up to me. He put his arm around my shoulders and said, 'I have waited for you, all my life.' The parents exploded with laughter. So did I. So did he. He was the son of a Russian mother and Italian father. He wanted to become an actor and had enough temperament for ten. Ever since then we had all been friends, his family and me and Mummy. Like Yvette, he had black curls and eyes.

Aunty came up to me on the park bench and said, still in a cold voice, 'We are going home now. Straight to bed.'

That night my stockings looked like dead snakes on the chair in the bedroom. Aunty had been sleeping with me the last week, and this made me feel nervous. Now, she was in the bathroom and I could look at myself in the bedroom mirror, unobserved. Angrily scratching the new hard bobble off the pimple, I wondered why lately I had felt totally happy one minute, and desperately miserable and lonely the next. I was always tired.

Aunty came in. Still silent and hurt, pale in her white flannel nightie, she looked short-sighted without glasses. I felt guilty and bad.

'I'm going to sleep in the other room. Good-night. Try and learn to be more considerate to those who do so much for you. Tonight was embarrassing and disgraceful.'

A weight seemed to want to lift, as she closed the door, yet I couldn't shrug the bad feelings off completely, so I told myself they were all ignorant, unfair, grown-ups. Suddenly I felt light and giddy. I started dancing in front of the mirror.

'I'm a film star,' I said to the mirror. 'I'm gorgeous, I'm Elizabeth Taylor. This country is stupid. Children only allowed into Walt Disney stuff, not movies, like in England. I'm beautiful and I can dance like Fred Astaire. He and Danny Kaye would like to marry me. The world is being deprived if they don't let me dance. I'll show them! I'll be famous one day. Everybody will love me.' I curtsied to my imaginary audience and heard them applauding me.

Suddenly I saw how ridiculous I was. After sticking my tongue out at my reflection I let myself fall over backwards on to the bed. Sitting up I smiled again deciding that it did look nice and that I should smile all the time.

'I'm a little lovely girl.' I hugged myself and talked like a baby. 'I am. I'm a little lovely girl. My Mummy and my Daddy are smiling faces, warm bodies, strong arms and kind voices. They dote on me and absolutely adore me. Can't be without me. They laugh and love my pranks. They have the power to charm away my fears and everything bad, make me feel wanted, and good and safe. They make me feel loved. Then why am I crying?'

'Olivia, what are you making such a noise for? What's the matter? Hans, Hans, get a flannel with cold water. She's suffocating! There, there, I didn't mean to scold you. Didn't mean to upset you so. Just cry it out gently. Gently. But try to stop crying if it . . . Olivia! Olly! Do calm down.'

Finally I regained control, but for a while I thought I was going to die for lack of air. Big sobs, like I'd never known before, shook my whole body. They took over. I had no control, grew panic-stricken at the force of them, ripping me apart.

Slowly, very slowly, I regained some calm. For the first time I was swept under, as though by a wave, by thoughts and questions I hadn't known were in me.

'We are all precious people in this world, aren't we? All of us precious, whether we're famous or not? Why don't Mummy and Daddy love me? Why did they always leave me or hurt me? Why?'

'Shush! They do love you. Your mother loves you very much, I know. She told me, often. Your daddy did so, too, in his own way, but he was ill, a poor sick man. He didn't know how to show feelings. We care too. Hans and I. Now, now, that's better. Smile! Come on, is there a smile there for me? That's better. Now just relax and I'll go and make a hot milk with honey for you. The Swiss honey you love, with black bread and butter.'

'Aunty Elly, shouldn't we all be kind and loving to one another? I mean, why did Mother suddenly love Andreas better than her husband? Why did Father do what he did? And where is he now? Why are there wars and why did my parents separate for all those war years? I mean, if there is a God and we are all important enough to Him, for Him to make this whole world, just for us, the whole universe, the sun, moon, stars, animals and flowers just for us . . . even butterflies, I mean imagine the strength He gave to ants to clean up whole carcasses, imagine the tiny muscles on fleas, and the force in snowdrops to push up through lumps of hard, frozen soil. All the plan behind it all! If all that works for . . . for billions of years, just for us, why don't we all love each other, simply and all the time?'

Aunty just looked at me and then as though she had gone suddenly shy, she stroked over my parting.

Hugging my knees, I said, 'I'm sorry if I was inconsiderate and naughty. You see, it's hard to explain, but always if I have the feeling that love stops flowing from the others to me, I can't seem to reach them with mine. I feel cut off. I feel hated. One day at the seaside – it was the first time I saw the sea – Daddy threw a big stone at me. Deliberately. It hit me on the side of my face. And that made me remember how every time I smuggled my doll into bed with me, and he found it, he'd come and bash its porcelain head on to mine, till I woke up, crying. Mummy crying too, somewhere, and that day at the sea, it was as if the tide had suddenly stopped rolling, the wind had suddenly stopped blowing, as if the birds fell dead and silent. I can't explain. Since then it's often been like that, like I was falling headlong into something terrible.

'And it was always like that with them. Whenever I felt happy, something terrible happened to squash my feelings flat. I called it "disappointment time". It seemed to last forever. As if I'd never feel glad again. It spoilt the memories of happy times too.'

'We all go through that, Olly. All the time. Life's like that. But I'm sure there are lots of happy times in store for you. Your life is only just beginning.' She kissed me and went to bed. I touched where she'd kissed me and couldn't go to sleep. After a while, I got up and fetched my diary and a pen. Writing always seemed to help. . . .

> I've lived in this world for 14 years and a half. That's 14 times 12 plus six – 174 months. Tomorrow I'll work out times 52 weeks, times 7 days, times 24 hours, times 60 minutes.
>
> Some of these times, Mummy and Daddy were smiling faces. Mummy more than Daddy. Daddy. To think he was the same man at Christmas, when he made that music-box for me. It was a round, clear cream wooden box. He polished it and worked on it for hours. He fitted the lid with a groove, where a tiny metal pole could be pushed up and when this was pulled down to open the lid, it triggered the music machinery and

started to play, to prevent robbers from opening it! He had been so pleased at how it turned out and it had been so beautifully crafted. And the same Christmas he had made one for Mummy and had given me a wind-up 'His Master's Voice' gramophone with Tchaikovsky's first and second piano concertos, plus the record of the Teddy Bears' Picnic . . . I should stop biting my fingernails. I wonder why Mummy and Daddy stopped talking and smiling?

I'm tired. I'll roll over and go to sleep now. It won't disturb Aunty now, if I roll and the bed-springs screech.

Chapter Six

The day Mummy arrived, I jumped out of bed with a loud Swiss 'Juhuiii!'

Andreas came to pick me up at ten. I was ready in my best clothes, with a dab of Aunty's makeup on the four new pimples on my chin.

As we drove to the airport I was sure either I or Mummy would have to die before we met. Surely this was too good to be happening? Then suddenly she stood in front of us – smiling. I'd forgotten how beautiful she was.

'Mummy!' I rushed up and hugged her.

'Schatzeli,' she said, as we kissed and squeezed each other tight. She went to hug Andreas.

'Where's Glen, Mummy? Where's Glen?'

'I left him in Ilkley, with the Clarks.'

Andreas said, 'I'm sure you're dying for your first strong Swiss coffee with croissants. Come on. Let's go to the restaurant after we collect your baggage.'

I walked along behind them. The real me lay crumpled up on the floor, hiding my face, crying – but 'Mother's me' dare not show my real feelings, only the ones I was expected to feel and permitted to show. I knew this well; it had always been like this.

'How long it has been, my Schatzeli. Yes, a *caffe complet*, please, with jam and Swiss cheese and Swiss butter, unsalted at last! How wonderful!' She held one hand of mine and one of Andreas. She smiled at us. I loved her hands. Boyish, practical and yet sort of helpless all in one.

She looked searchingly into my eyes. Testing me.

'Schatzeli?'

I smiled. Prayed. Cramped away my tears.

'Are you so pleased to see me, dearling?'

I had to laugh at the familiar old mistake when she mixed up 'dear' and 'darling'. She stroked my cheek. She looked at Andreas, and they both didn't see the tears now rolling, and

I managed to hide them well while eating.

As I tried to fall asleep that first night after Mummy arrived, guilt engulfed me because I hated myself and was sorry for myself. I was so angry and upset that I would never see my dog again, I could not stop crying. Andreas had told me not to spoil Mummy's homecoming because of the dog.

I'd try to be good and pleasant, try to push away the constant heaviness I felt.

This was a nagging, pulling weight which made me heave, gulp and sigh in terror whilst trying to fall asleep.

At the dinner table at Aunty's, Mummy had said, 'Fancy, you still have that habit of sighing heavily during eating. I hope you'll grow out of it.'

'I didn't notice it,' I said. 'I don't notice in the daytime.'

They rented a flat near the surgery. It had a long corridor. Andreas had organised everything and all we needed was there. A new life together, I thought.

I wasn't allowed to mention Glen as Mummy said she was just as sad without a dog, had always had one, and the parting from Glenny had been dreadful for her.

After two weeks it was arranged that I would stay with Aunty Elly again, for the day. She was in one of her cold huffs.

'Just got your things and went, once Mother was back, but now it's convenient to plonk you on to me again.'

I didn't know where to look, or how to behave. She brought me back at six. As the door of our new apartment opened, on my return, an Airedale puppy, high on long legs, ran up and away. Up and down the long polished corridor it ran, losing its balance, falling, oversized snout onto paws, struggling up only to slip and skid again. As I ran in delight towards it, Andreas came up and asked, 'How do you like the new dog I got your mother? His name's Rex. He's a pedigree. Isn't he fantastically beautiful and comic?'

Mummy just couldn't stop beaming at the newcomer.

Later we left him in the new bed. They had purchased everything for his well-being. We went out for a meal.

Mummy was pleased and said, 'We've achieved much in these two first weeks. A new home, a new dog and now a wonderful new finishing school for you, Olivia.' I dropped my spoon into the soup.

'Tomorrow we're driving you to Gstaad to look at it. It's the newest, most expensive, exclusive *Institute des jeunes filles* in Switzerland.'

'Tomorrow?'

'Only to look at, dearling. Your father's firm is paying. You have to go there. You see, it's not my decision. Your father's firm and the law think me unfit to bring you up, after. . . . You need young people, young girls of your own age. You'll be very happy there. I know. You should be very grateful for such a wonderful opportunity.' She looked sad.

'Mummy! You unfit! You're the most wonderful mother in the world. They can't take me away from you? I know what a good mother you are. I'll tell them.'

She looked at me and smiled sorrowfully. Andreas, looking on was touched and placed his big, pink, surgical paw, covered with freckles, over her small, tanned hand.

'We have no choice, Schatz,' he said. 'All those narrow-minded people out there, who judge us and are jealous, think we live in sin and are immoral and unfit for you. You have to go.'

Mummy said, 'Other girls! Friends! Skiing! Mountain air plus a good general education will be a blessing for you.'

I saw no way out. Another goodbye.

Once more a dog could stay and I had to go.

Chapter Seven

Gstaad! The name alone was impossible to say.

They told me the Duke of Kent went to school there, at 'Les Rosays', and many film stars and famous people. That I'd make friendships, valuable for life, with high society girls from all over the world. Didn't that sound exciting?

It didn't mean a thing. Only new pain, new separation and more rejection.

We drove via Thun, Spiez and Zweisimmen to Gstaad. Hard as I tried not to be impressed, the mountains, the lakes and villages with the chalets were breathtaking. We found our way to the *Institute des jeunes filles*. It was an enormous, sun-scorched wooden chalet of three storeys. Pink and red flowers in carved boxes hung from all the balconies, which faced white gleaming mountains in the blazing sun. For a second I thought of sooty Bradford.

A lady opened the door. The hall was grand: wood panels painted with roses; chests and wardrobes matching; paintings and carvings and antiques wherever we looked.

Madame smiled and looked warm-hearted, so I dared say, 'Mummy, please ask her about not forcing me to eat.'

'Dummerli!'

Apologising, Mummy explained in French that I was afraid of being forced to eat after a bad childhood experience.

Turning to me, Madame said kindly, 'Here there will be nothing to be afraid of. You eat or you don't eat. Just as much as you feel like. You serve yourself and take what you want.'

Suddenly the door burst open. A handsome young man in a pale-blue shirt rushed in. 'Ah! *Excusez-moi, Madame, mais . . .*'

He turned to us and I was conscious of his blue eyes, the bluest I'd ever seen. He said, smiling brightly, 'I don't like your hair but I missed you.'

I gaped. Everyone smiled politely. I had just had my first perm and felt very self-conscious. Wondering why he'd said such a strange thing, I asked, 'Why don't you like my hair?'

There was relieved laughter on all sides as the misunderstanding was cleared up. He'd said, in his Dutch accent, 'I ran like a hare, but I missed you.'

Having understood that we were to arrive by train, he had run in vain to meet us at the station.

The four other girls being interviewed this day looked more grown-up than I did. We could only smile and say our names, as we were all from different countries. The main language of the school was French.

It was decided that I would come to stay in three weeks. First, much had to be purchased and everything tagged with my name. I was almost looking forward to being part of this beautiful and relaxed school atmosphere. We loved the bedrooms with their own bathrooms and balconies, and the studio for gymnastics. It seemed an astounding school. Mother said, 'See, Olly! Mother always knows best!' She gave me a loving squeeze.

Madame was saying, 'She will need ice skates and skis and good boots, but skiing-trousers, pullovers and anoraks will be school uniform and can be ordered here. It's all *bleu, blanc, rouge. Vive la France!* She will also need evening dress for the balls at other schools and at the Palace Hotel. Also other sportswear, depending on whether she'll ride or play tennis or hockey.' My eyes must have begun to shine, yet I still felt nervous and apprehensive. How was I going to manage all this, I wondered, as I looked at the handsome teacher who had been introduced as Mr Ivo van Landers.

Madame seemed rushed, so we soon left. As we drove back to Basel, I felt much better than at the beginning of the day.

Three weeks later I was once more at the school and being greeted by my new teacher.

'Hello, young Swiss miss from Yorkshire,' he said, blinding me with his smile. 'I'm to take you for private French lessons each morning, to help you catch up in the language. In two or three weeks a new French mistress will be here for grammar and conversation. I'll take over the literature, then. Molière, La Fontaine, Victor Hugo, Sartre, André Gide – the old and the classic. It's all great stuff.'

How I longed for that lesson, every day, and how I worked! He was pleased with my progress, and an inspiring teacher to work with. He looked wonderful and smelled of spicy after-shave. Above all, he really seemed to like me.

One day he asked me, 'Why are you so depressed, some mornings? You look pale and worried today.'

It was as if he'd hit me. He'd stop liking me! I must make an effort to be witty and cheerful. Often I tried hard to make people laugh. When they didn't respond I would feel dumb and convinced I was not an intelligent, likable person. With some girls it all came so naturally. Everyone loved their company.

'I just don't sleep very well,' I said, and then started to decline my French verbs.

But the nights grew worse and I slept less and less. I was now afraid of falling asleep, because of the bad dreams. To while away the time, I would escape into wild fantasies about Ivo van Landers and myself. He would rescue me from earthquakes and floods, hurricanes, fires and avalanches, would carry me to safety and then dress my wounds and put me to bed. He'd always hold me close and comfort me. Eventually I'd fall asleep, exhausted, at three or four in the morning, only to wake, crying and shaking, some two hours later. Dawn would find me rushing to my bathroom, dabbing cold water on my swollen eyes, wanting desperately to look nice for him at our lesson after breakfast.

It took more and more effort to control the shaking of my hands and the sudden compulsion to cry. One morning it happened. . . . My vocabulary was not learned. My verbs were bad, and I could still not understand the *participe passé*. Ivo grew impatient. I burst into tears. Astounded at the intensity of my reaction, which I could not suppress, he rushed over to me.

'What have I done? What is the matter? I mean, you are here to learn and I am trying to help you so that you can communicate better with the other girls and teachers. But you must do your part. You started off so well, but lately you're learning less and less. Are you feeling all right?'

'No!' I howled. 'I can't sleep and I don't feel well.' Feeling ashamed, I continued, 'I can't sleep and if I do, I have this horrible dream, again and again.'

He came to sit next to me. 'Tell me about it. Dreams will help others to help you. Go on.'

A fly was buzzing and banging against the windowpane.

I looked down on a sheet of paper in front of me, where I'd scribbled circles and lines, black and thick.

'Go on,' he coaxed gently. So I began. . . .

'Every time I fall asleep, I am this tiny little kitten. I'm so small that I fear getting trodden on. I begin to walk around. I'm in the high green grass of a summer meadow. It smells lovely. The butterflies hover on buttercups and daisies, above me. As I watch them from below, I wish, in my dream, to stay here. For nothing to change this peace, or hurt me, just as I wouldn't dream of harming the butterflies. I walk along. The thick grass strokes and tickles the sides of my furry belly. I even press myself flat against the ground, stretching out my front paws. Clawing the earth, I pull myself along. I roll over and feel the sun on my white tummy. I feel totally free. Relaxed.

'And then I hear it! Then things start to get spoilt, every time. The thudding! I can hear the thudding. I jump and crouch and hide and wait for it. The pounding of it and the running makes me scared. I get so scared that I start to run, but it chases me. I dash away until I come to a huge, empty swimming pool. There is no time to run round it, so I have to jump. It's deep and it hurts as I fall, crashing headlong into darkness. Limping in pain into a corner, I see concrete all around me! I'm trapped! That's when he jumps on top of me! It's awful. It's the wolf! His teeth snatch, his claws rip. The stench of his yellow teeth and bad breath are in my face, ready to devour me. I beg him not to harm me, say I'll do anything.'

' "Anything?" he growls, and it echoes round me.

' "Yes, anything," I say.

'So he takes me by the scruff of my neck and pulls me into the centre of the huge arena. "Eat this, then!" he barks. I see a great plate of soup. It is green and slimy and it stinks. I have to sit at the edge and suck it in. Lap it up. Eat it.

' "Swallow the stuff!" he yells, and as he does, a snake begins to turn its head towards me, from the middle of the soup. It starts to swim towards me. I know it wants to get inside my mouth. I begin to retch and choke. Just as it's going to strangle me and force its way down my throat, I wake up.

'I'm gagging and near vomiting; I shake and cry and sweat. I can't stop. Can't go back to sleep. Oh, Mr van Landers, this happens all the time! I don't only feel frightened, but I feel so dumb. Mummy would call me hysterical. All the other girls here seem so happy . . . so normal . . . so adult. I feel stupid and alone beside them.'

Ivo had listened gravely.

'Olivia. Come to my study at five, after afternoon tea. I'll have something ready for you. Now, one thing. I want you to promise me to write down the dreams immediately after you wake up. Write them down. Tell yourself that you're writing it out of your system. It's all part of growing up. Say to yourself, I'll talk it over with Mr van Landers tomorrow. He'll explain. Tell yourself it's normal, all part of maturing. Digesting the past and coming to terms with the present. It's nothing to be afraid or ashamed of. I will help you to understand yourself, and it's O.K.'

The fly found a way out. I heaved a sigh of relief. He said, 'D'you feel better now? You see, the kitten is you. In your own eyes you're still insignificant and unimportant. But you're the wolf too. You'll be able to be big and strong and scary too. You're the author of your own dreams. They are just stories. Don't let them worry you.' As he said this, he gave me a nudge on the side of my cheek with the front, flat, side of his fist, sort of friendly, half gentle, half rough.

In my room I remembered this gesture. I felt again the touch. It made me tingle warmly all over, and a little spurt of happiness burst somewhere deep inside. That night I was less afraid. I had someone! Someone who listened and cared. Someone who had offered to help. I suddenly felt so tremendous that I threw on my tracksuit and went for a run. I laughed out loud as I leapt and bounded along. I waved to the mountains and in spite of feeling a little foolish, whispered 'Old as the hills! My new friends. I remember my sunrise with Grosspapa on you.'

In the gold-framed mirror in the hall, I saw my reflection – red cheeks and sparkling eyes.

'You look pretty tonight,' he said, and I could have sung and danced.

That evening he gave me a leather-bound book to write in. On the first page he had written, in his fastidiously neat, tiny writing.

1. I am a unique, valuable person. Every person is.
2. I should never compare myself with others. I am me.
3. I must learn to love and accept myself.

4. If I can't love myself, I can't love others.
5. My attitude towards life, makes life.
6. I must learn to live in the present.
7. To learn to know myself is the greatest art and honesty.
8. Out of every death new life grows.
9. I am part of everyone. Everyone is part of me.
10. I have a teacher and a friend who believes in me.

Ivo van Landers

In my room, I pressed the book to my cheek again and again. That night I slept soundly.

From then on, I began to settle in. I made progress with my French and I dared to try and talk at the table. The mistakes caused much laughter and we girls all began to feel more at ease with each other. I could look around and say to myself, look at this picture: all these girls and people, living together in such beautiful surroundings. Keep it in your mind, for one day it will be only a memory. Enjoy it now and make the best of it all.

The only punishing thing in my life, now, was my menstrual period. It had started when I was twelve and Father was still alive. I used to use it as an excuse not to have to go to bed with him. He couldn't even believe me the first times and always wanted proof. I had felt nauseatingly ashamed as he had insisted, in his brutal way, that I pull down my pants. He used to stare so. Once he knew the date, I couldn't cheat much. He'd always ask to check. There was no room for privacy anywhere.

I still felt humiliated and ashamed, every month. Dirty, inferior, but worst of all, I passed out with the pain. The cramps were so terrible that the doctor had once said, '*Un petit accouchement*.' Every time! I found it such a humiliating telltale. I'd have to go to bed for one or two days. I missed out on so much fun, and of course it was always when a fabulous outing was planned, or when we wanted to go swimming, riding or skiing. I hated being a woman. I often told God I thought he could have let it come out from under our arms, or at least without pain, and only for an hour or two.

But I loved being a woman again when we started dancing! On our first wobbly high heels, we girls seemed to spend every spare moment dancing together. We practised the waltz, the tango, samba, mambo, Charleston, foxtrot, boogie-woogie and later the Madison. There was music in the air, mixing and mingling from all rooms, balconies and levels: *Begin the Beguine, Do you know Miss Jones?, La cucaracha, J'attendrais toujours, Oh sole mio, My funny Valentine, Peg o' my heart, Stormy weather,* and a song we made up called, *Sweet sixteen and never been kissed*. My life began to be sunny and pleasant. A mixture of fun, tunes, languages, rhythm and sport. The great old chalet was our stage, the snowy slopes of the surrounding mountains our wider setting. The skiing highlighted our days at first, adding great excitement. Later, as the sport continued to be a must, it began to be a bore. Skiing a bore! I'd laugh at that in later years.

Chapter Eight

I read Nietzsche, Kant and Hegel. Schopenhauer, Plato, Socrates, Descartes, Sartre, Shakespeare, Hugo and Molière. I didn't understand all of what these great philosophers were saying. I got mad at the insult of Nietzsche, 'When you go to a woman, don't forget your whip,' and was glad to hear he had syphilis and went mad. I thought about Ivo incessantly. He was my hero. And slowly my nightmares were replaced by dreams about him. I read all these books to impress him. To ask and talk and discuss.

As Ivo began to overestimate me, expecting me to follow long, tiring lectures, during which I tried hard to look intelligent, it grew more and more difficult to keep it all up. In the end I was a sponge that soaked itself, unquestioningly, full of his thoughts, his words, his ideas and theories.

One day we had an afternoon of pottery and clay modelling. An Italian girl sculptured a most beautiful Madonna. She was a Japanese-looking Madonna, emerging from a lotus flower. Her creator probably had been influenced by Ivo's Eastern philosophy courses. I was perplexed at the simple beauty this girl had created. Later, it hurt me to see Ivo taking it in his hand, and with a fine stick, altering a bit here and a bit there, until the whole figure had changed. It had become his.

Probably I surprised myself more than anybody else by the raging anger that swept away all of my self-control on this occasion. I burst into tears, shouting about the despicable crime teachers committed who were too full of themselves to accept that someone else was good at something too. I shouted that he had murdered the Madonna, had committed a terrible crime.

The silence! The shame! I ran to my room, crying. I didn't understand or recognise myself.

I didn't dare descend for the evening meal, but when I thought everybody was at the dinner table, I slipped out for a breath of fresh air. The crisply crunching snow sounded wrong in comparison to my depressed mood. I saw the silent, dark silhouettes of the mountains. . . . Suddenly I came to with a start. Ivo had stepped out from under a tree.

We stood still. He blew out the smoke of a cigarette in the sighing way he affected when he was pensive. He just stood in my way. I dared not move.

'I don't know what's the matter with me,' he said. 'You were completely right, of course.'

So taken aback was I at him being the one to apologise, that a sob broke out of me.

'I'm the one who doesn't know what's the matter with me, and I'm deeply sorry,' I whispered, a frog rasping in my throat.

For a split second he drew me close. My face rested on the rough material of his jacket. I could smell his after-shave, like cinnamon, mingled with his cigarette smoke and the snowy air. My knees went weak. I could hear his heart. I shivered. It reminded me of being on Mother's lap when I was small and of being frightened in case her heart beat would stop and she'd die.

I heard chairs being pushed back, the clatter of feet, dishes and plates. Three girls came tearing out of the back door, which banged and screeched on its hinges. Like a scared rabbit, I raced away. Where should I go? I couldn't go to my room with a face so flushed and a heart ready to burst. I hurried up the path behind the chalet until I was out of breath. The collar of my big coat was rubbing my neck sore. I almost welcomed this, told myself I wasn't allowed to turn it down, then later realised I was an idiot and adjusted it to be comfortable.

'You can't walk about all night,' I scolded myself out loud. 'Look at yourself! Melodrama. Who d'you think you are? Lady Chatterley? Oh, shut up! Go home!'

On the way home, I told myself he was sorry. So what? It's nice of him. A good trait. Now behave normally. Put it all out of your mind and forget it.

I walked into the house and up the stairs. Here the familiar picture of girls reassured me for the moment. Girls with curlers, girls in dressing-gowns with glasses of milk, girls in groups, some passing on the stairs, others standing and talking, the ones who were always in a rush squeezing and clattering past the others.

I entered our room. There again, girls everywhere. Two English friends, Sally and Fiona, lay sprawled across our beds, painting the nails on each other's toes and fingers. On the gramophone a Charleston was blaring and three French girls and Graziella were flinging their limbs all over the place, as if their lives depended on their dancing. I walked into the bathroom. Penny, Coco and Gabriella were sitting in the tub, concentrating on squeezing out each others pimples and blackheads.

'I feel ugly today. Positively u-g-l-y! Please, someone, tell me that I'm not. P-l-e-a-s-e!' Somewhere, someone was yelling this at the top of her voice, and from round about a few other girls joined in a mock chorus. 'You're beautiful! You're beau-won-fabulous!'

It was a game we played when one of us felt ugly. We had decided that all women had these moments. That when we had our periods, it was like being out of control, like a baby piss-poohing its nappies. But a baby wouldn't feel ugly at these times, so why should we? Why shouldn't we be able to bawl about it and reassure each other? I felt better now.

'Where've you been?' my French room-mate demanded. 'We were going to listen to the third Beethoven piano concerto tonight. Remember? Yes?' I loved her French accent.

'Yes, Magda, I haven't forgotten. We shall listen if this crowd will let us appreciate some culture and pipe down!' Someone threw a pillow at me. I retaliated and a wild battle started.

A loud knock brought us up with a start. Then a bell sounded. Our friends trooped off to their rooms. We switched on the radio and listened. 'He plays the introduction too slowly,' said my genius. I snuggled into bed.

I didn't see Ivo for a week. He had the flu. Then I came down with it too. After recovering, he treated me coolly. It stung. I was mad with myself, because he managed to be on my mind constantly.

Madame was pleasant, yet she seemed to prefer the more elegant girls. She organised fashion parades. The French and Italian girls won prizes for their Dior and Balenciaga models. I called it ridiculous and unfair, called them cows on the market parading the best udders. Some of us made fun of them mercilessly. We said the cows in the meadows round our chalets had eyes more docile and intelligent, declared that their ornamented cow-bells would suit the girls better than the jewellery these young students wore. We were so nasty because we agreed that Madame was 'cultivating inferiority complexes'.

As if clothes and jewels were so important!

Monsieur Belmont was a cold, strict man. He had a naked look about him and he always stared through me. His narrow, bald head reminded me of a penis.

Our new French mistress was a typical spinster. Fussy! Infuriating! She brought out the cruelty in us. The poor old thing was a convenient object with which to prove our superiority. '*Pauvre Mademoiselle*!' She didn't last long. She'd scratch at her ugly patches of bleeding eczema on arms, legs and face, while screeching at us in her parrot voice, only to be ignored completely.

I sat at the back in Ivo's classes. We were now sixty girls, split into groups of ten. Our private lessons were over. I tried to regain his attention through thoughts in my compositions. At last, he wrote, under one of my stories, 'How can a young person of your few years think so deeply and ask questions and find answers worthy of some of the greatest thinkers like Montaigne? I congratulate you, especially as it is so refreshingly simply presented. Good work! Keep it up. As you know, I criticise the intellectuals who write in such a complicated manner that the average person cannot understand.'

I glowed and worked even harder, learning to debate and argue just for the fun of it, for the 'brain-gymnastics'!

And suddenly it was just the two of us again. Aware of it occasionally I'd blush and stop in the middle of a sentence. If I sat near him at table, we'd forget everything around us. We'd sit there, still deep in conversation after all the others had gone. One Saturday we were still talking when the others came back for afternoon tea. We'd talked from lunch time on. No one was more surprised than we were.

This was my most beautiful time of learning. Free and easy. We had reached a new level of challenging each other's thoughts. In time Magda, Penny and Sally joined in the debates, but they grew tired of it quickly.

Then again he started to ignore me.

I couldn't think what I'd done wrong.

I grew so desperate that I put a note into my exercise book, along with my homework. 'What have I done? Why are you cross with me?'

Breathlessly I went to get my book back, the week after.

'Nothing! All is well! I know now why I paid such special

attention to you. You see, you remind me of a sister I had, who died very young. She drowned while skating. I must not favour you because of that. It is not fair on others. Monsieur warned me. Girls began to notice. I'm sorry. I was unaware.'

I went to cry and lick my wounds.

So that was the only reason he liked me. I was nothing to him and would be one of the crowd from now on. I could hardly bear the following weeks as he joked more with the others and hardly had a word for me.

After a yoga lecture I wrote about a strange experience I'd had. I had gone to bed and tried to do a meditation exercise he had told us about. I had fallen into a sort of trance and then seen a fire, like the petals of a red flower, through which I glimpsed God. This image had stayed still, as no other thought or image ever had. I had felt at peace and one with the Universe. I had felt as if my teacher and I were one person.

Underneath the essay, Ivo wrote, 'This is most astounding, for exactly at the same time, on the same night, I was doing the same exercise and I had the same experience. I would like to talk about it. Can I meet you at the Olden at five?'

At the Olden! Me! The Olden was the nicest hotel in the village, famous for its painted shutters and facade, known for its food and the owner, who sang and played the piano. It was out of bounds for us. We were only permitted to go with parents, teachers or authorised adults. Some teachers went there to discuss exams with older girls. I felt most fortunate for being granted this favour, and prepared with great care for the rendezvous.

I saw him. It took my breath away and I wondered why. We sat in the cosy, sombre room, beneath the low-beamed ceiling. Music played in the background. We ordered tea and coffee and dried mountain meat. We loved this specialty. Paper-thinly sliced meat which had been hung to dry in the air and sun, in a loft. *Viande des Grisons*!

'You and your tea!' he teased. 'That's all you need to make you happy, isn't it?'

'Yes.' I beamed. (And you, I thought.)

'Now then,' he began. He looked frighteningly serious. 'I have missed you. I do like your hair! And I've missed you.' I was touched that he remembered that first misunderstanding, of our first meeting.

'You are so beautiful. So pure, little girl.'

I was baffled. Had I heard right or was it a new misunderstanding?

He had mumbled, but now he resumed, loudly, 'Now, down to business. How often and how long have you been meditating and how often do you see the lotus flower?'

'I didn't know I had seen it,' I answered. 'What I saw was just so peaceful and so beautiful that I wanted to describe it. Nothing like that has ever happened to me before – or after.'

'You must be very spiritually gifted. A very special person. I love the way you think, in comparison to all those superficial, spoilt girls. They are only concerned with money, clothes, jewellery, boys and makeup. If there is one thing I hate, it's red fingernails and red trousers. I don't know why, but I hate it. One of the Americans said to me, the other day, that she was going to marry rich husbands. Do you hear? *Husbands* – a few of them! In order to divorce them for mental cruelty, to live a wealthy, extravagant life, as she put it!'

'I know. They have strange ideas.'

'You're so refreshingly genuine, and you think. You're the only one wanting to go on with algebra and geometry.'

'That's only because I want to conquer what I don't understand.' (And be with you, I thought.)

'That's a great reason and you're a great kid. I enjoy talking to you more than to all the teachers, too. Only Patsy O'Neill. She's a wonderful person and d'you know what? You and Magda are her favourite pupils and Sally. But don't get ideas! I'm only telling you because of that old inferiority complex of yours I helped chase away! I know you won't get big-headed.'

I was so pleased, and sitting there with him felt so good, that I wanted it to go on forever.

'Now, I have a confession to make, but maybe you will never forgive me.'

'You? A confession to me?'

'Yes. And it's very hard but I've got to tell you. You see, I tried to ignore you, because I liked you much too much and I . . . I thought you might get teased or into trouble. I, I didn't know how to handle it. I'm sorry. I know it hurt you, so I want to explain, specially as it's your birthday in a few days.'

'How do you know about my birthday?'

'That would be telling! Surprise, surprise.'

I felt a surge of excitement.

'I understand,' I said, 'about you ignoring me because of your little sister. I'm terribly sorry and sad about that. It must have been dreadful.'

'Well, that's part of my confession. I made that up. I just didn't know how to account for always wanting to be with you. You're fifteen and I'm thirty-two. And besides, you have your whole life in front of you, and it's all wrong. So today I thought I would talk about all this with you. Clear it up and start anew as good friends.' With this he placed a small parcel in front of me.

'Open it at home,' he said. 'Now I must go, and we'll take it from here. You're a great kid, Olivia. The greatest, and I'm more than fond of you. You'll grow up to be a fine lady and I envy the man who will marry you. I've got to go and do some shopping, so I'll let you go up to school alone. And remember, from now on we're friends.'

'Friends forever, I hope,' I said, and rushed off unnecessarily hurriedly.

I ran all the way back. Once in the chalet, I ran to a toilet to open my present. It was a Pestalozzi Diary, a page for every day, crowned with a thought by this great Swiss educator and thinker. Into the front Ivo had written, 'To my very special pupil, friend and "inspiration". I am grateful just because you are in my life.'

Into the page for my birthday, the ninth of March, he had stuck a wee parcel in tissue paper. Eagerly I opened it. A tiny pendant of a moonstone on a silver chain! Sitting in that confining room, I could have yelled out. Suddenly such happiness surged through me, as I never knew existed. I flushed the water just to be able to laugh loudly. My cheeks burned when I washed my hands at the basin. I hardly recognised my eyes, they looked so big and staring. I put on my chain, grateful no one had come in. I hugged the air, then myself. I had to breathe in great gulps.

Magda, always at her piano, looked up in startled surprise when I raced into the room, jumped out of my skirt into trousers, tore them off as I remembered how he hated red ones, then pulled on my grey ones, rushing as if pursued.

'Magda, come for a run! Come on!' I danced round her, hassling.

'Come on! You'll get notes in your brain and get fat and grow old quickly. Come on!'

'Laisse moi! Tu es folle! Complètement folle! One day you are melancholy, the next you burst with joy! Womens! God explain how you made womens!'

'I love the way you say "melancholy" and "womens". I love you! I must run, work off some energy, or else I'll explode.'

'Olly, *que tu es drôle*. Off with you then. Leave me in peace!'

That night in bed I asked her, 'Have you ever been in love?'

She said, 'Yes. In Paris. Near home. But he not even knows I am alive. But now it is agonising. I have what you call this . . . a crush? Driving me insane. That is why I need to play the piano all the time. It is a secret, but I must tell you. I am miserably in love with Ivo.'

I was glad we'd talked in the dark, relieved I hadn't said what had been so pressing to get out, that day.

From then on I noticed, as if I was awake to life in a new way, that every woman had her eyes on Ivo. Be it at the cinema, at an outing to a hotel for a ball, a concert or fondue dinner by candlelight, or skiing. Wherever we went, the ladies would look at him in that special way.

Soon it was the ninth of March. It was a Sunday. The whole school knew my birthday surprise and wanted me out of the way, so a few were organised to take me to church. When we came back, Madame called me into the dining room. There was a huge cake with candles and a pile of presents! Then – Mummy!

Open-mouthed, I stood and stared. Everyone burst into laughter and squeals of delight. We were in each other's arms.

'Mummy! What a lovely surprise!'

'Olly! How well you look. Isn't this nice? I can stay for a week.'

I just couldn't believe this was happening.

Every single girl had given me a present. As they all knew I was horse crazy, I got horse posters, porcelain horses, carved wooden horses, books on horses and paintings of horses. One was a photo-book called *All the happiness on earth is on the back of a horse*. From Mummy I got my first jodhpurs, riding-hat and *abonnement* for ten lessons, also a sweet yellow and black evening dress with a sash and puffy little sleeves. It was cut quite low! There was a pair of high heels to go with it! Also a pink lipstick and my first Ponds cold cream!

I kept hugging and laughing. As I jumped round in my excitement, a French girl said, 'You'll never be a lady, always stay a kid.' This sobered me immediately. For about ten minutes I behaved more posed, then I thought, I'm me, and if I'm not the posed type, to blazes with it!

All day the excitement was nearly too much. We all went to see a film in the afternoon, *La Symphonie Pastorale* with Michelle Morgan. It was sad.

In the evening Patsy O'Neill arranged dinner out for Mother and me and Ivo. Every pupil had their favourite teachers. Monsieur and Madame liked the more elegant people. They smiled as we all trooped out. *'Bonne soirée! Bonne anniversaire!'*

That night, at the Olden, Ivo explained how he felt about me to Mummy. She didn't seem surprised. I looked from one to the other, thinking how much I loved them. We all drank wine and ate schnitzels with small noodles and salads. After the third bottle, Mummy asked, 'But what do you think will happen?'

Ivo answered, 'Do you want me to leave the school or do you want to place Olivia in a different institute somewhere else?'

I must have looked shocked.

'Oh, no!' Mother said. 'She hasn't been very lucky, nor happy. There were sad circumstances with my husband, the war, you know. Things didn't turn out well for her. She needs understanding and happiness. I'm so glad if she is so well and happy now. No. I trust you. I'm honoured and touched that you proposed to go. No. I entrust Olivia to you. Help to make her happy. Take away the . . . the wrong impressions she may have got. Maybe she was unnaturally awakened. You know her feelings. I don't know. Just be sensitive. You are the teacher. You have studied psychology. Just be . . .'

She took another sip and I heard Ivo ask, 'If she grows to really love me and when she is older, and wants it, would you consider me marrying Olivia?'

I sat very quietly. I didn't know if I liked this way of it all happening. Shouldn't we first have begun to talk about this alone, gradually? It was all so suddenly final and serious. An impending responsibility, not fun. Or was I immature? Oh, what on earth was I supposed to do? To feel?

Mother smiled at me fondly. I was proud, now, because she

saw how seriously this wonderful, clever person was taking me.

Mother said, 'I am grateful that you have not judged me by my past failures. I feel we understand each other and will never hurt each other. I feel all of us are kindred souls. Let's make *Schmollis*!'

They linked arms at the elbows and drank thus, intertwined, after which it is customary to kiss one another and call each other 'du' instead of 'sie'. Now it was Christian names and friends for life.

We all wobbled a bit as we walked out. Mrs Olden, at the piano, bowed her head and smiled. I felt very grand. I knew my new dress and high heels looked wonderful. Earlier in the evening, Ivo had stared when I'd walked in and had said, 'What a metamorphosis.' I hadn't known what it meant. Outside, I now stumbled and tripped. He caught me, and I said, 'Catch your memryphorsis.' He laughed.

We took Mother to her hotel room. She promised to be at the school before lunch. Ivo and I sauntered up the hill, past the Palace Hotel, all alone for the first time. We walked and held hands. He carried my flimsy shoes. I had on a thick coat and boots. The moon shone and we still wobbled and laughed. Under a tree, in the dark, he kissed me for the first time.

'I couldn't speak of my wish to marry you, yet. I'll tell you why, soon. I'm sorry. I just had to know how your mother felt. I felt so guilty about loving you so desperately. You, so young. I didn't know how you felt though your eyes told me. I love you, Olivia.'

'Oh, Ivo! Can this be happening to me? I've loved you ever since I saw you. Ever since your first words.'

'Which were a misunderstanding!' We huddled close and laughed.

'Oh, Ivo! I'm so happy.' I was. I had never felt anything like this. I looked up, for our lips had touched only briefly. I waited. He looked so beautiful. I closed my eyes and he said softly 'Mmmmmm' and then his lips met mine in a long kiss first quivering, then demanding and hungry. It was the most fantastic experience I had ever felt. I prayed for this never to stop. We kissed again and again.

'Oh, Ivo! Fifteen and never been kissed. Wow! Isn't that something!'

He chuckled quietly. I loved every sound he made.

But despite the closeness, or maybe because of it, we began

to shiver. 'C'mon, little 'un. I can't have you catching cold. Happy birthday, my little 'un.'

'Stop calling me that. I'm so near to twenty.'

'Sure. Sure. So near to twenty. Anyway, let's get you home. I'd love to tuck you in and some day I will.'

Magda was asleep. She'd been hurt that I didn't invite her. Something was happening to our friendship. It wasn't the same. I didn't feel as if I was the same person, there in bed beside her, that night. I was now a kissed person. A person demanded in marriage. A tiny bit overwhelmed and confused, I fell asleep.

The days that followed were some of our happiest ones – for Mummy and me, I mean.

Mummy sitting in sunny bedrooms with girls of all nations sprawled on beds around her. Mummy on balconies, in the sun. Mummy and girls smoking, talking, dancing. Even singing. Mummy inviting us all to Charlie's, buying us piles of cakes and teas. My mother at the fondue dinners, young and laughing, enjoying fun and music. Mummy and Ivo, the girls and me. Magda didn't join in for a while, but after a long talk we fell into each other's arms and made up. We went out to dinner once more, and invited her with Sally and Patsy and Ivo. We were very careful.

One day Mother was a fading, waving hand from a train window.

Then she was gone.

Chapter Nine

The notes, exchanged in my homework books, were turning into love letters, and suddenly, one evening, we were alone again, Ivo and I. He had found the key to a hut in the wood behind the chalet. The nights were now less cold. The hut had a hole in its roof. As we entered he drew me close. I looked up at this beautiful man, looked up at the stars, but as he whispered my name, a memory hit and stung. A memory of a little girl under the stars, having to hold Father's . . . Father, there . . . My aching arm . . . my stomach sick, under the sky. I pulled away and stiffened.

'What's the matter?'

I wanted to push him away, but I pushed away the memory instead. His lips met mine, unbelievably soft. Comforting. He pulled me nearer to him, gently, then more strongly, and I pressed to meet him. His mouth began to open – and I pulled back.

'Is something wrong, little one? I have longed for you so much.'

I still couldn't believe this was really happening. I wanted it, had dreamed of it, but now I was scared, proud, and yet confused. I suddenly wanted to go. I felt fed up with the whole thing, but I started to kiss, to prove that . . . I don't know . . . so as not to offend him, perhaps – to prove that I was 'normal', maybe.

I too now let my tongue explore gently, very cautiously. Suddenly I liked it again, and feelings like fireworks exploded in me – specially as he kissed my neck. I had a sense of being so safe and unalone. I grew limp, feeling weak with such strong waves of unknown emotions washing all over me, that I moaned. His hands caressed, waking the hunger in me to caress him, to give, to melt, eyes closed as if in a deep dream. But as his hands slid beneath my jumper, he felt me jump as he touched my breast. I shivered. He stopped.

'Sensitive, sexy little girl. You respond well. I like that.' I realised that this was what I was supposed to be. I felt sick.

He looked at me quizzically. 'My darling, I'll teach you. I'll wait. I'll be patient and gentle. I love you, my sweet one, my lovely, lovely little girl.'

That did it! I felt instantly guilty and I knew I felt so much for him. 'I love you, Ivo, so much it hurts. I shall never be able to tell you or show you.'

'I know. I can feel. You are so wonderful, darling.'

'Please kiss me again,' I heard myself begging, although I was not sure if I really wanted to get into this danger zone once more. 'I wish we'd never have to stop,' I told him, but I was not sure if I meant it. Smiling, he cuddled me anew. And suddenly I thought I knew that we belonged together. I believed now that I wanted to be his and that everything he did was right.

Again he began to stroke my breasts and I tried not to wince. 'We've always belonged together and we always will.' I hugged him tightly, as tightly as I could, to make pushing away his hand seem like an accident. He pushed me back and pulled up my jumper. I smiled, suppressing angry feelings. Why is he doing this?

'How pure,' he said. 'What pure, young, beautiful breasts in the moonlight. This is art worthy of a painter. I'm so proud of you.'

I didn't look down; I felt ashamed. I didn't want to see myself like that but I was proud he was proud of me.

Later I had to sneak to a toilet to rearrange myself. I was not sure whether I was glad or sorry it was over.

Magda was sound asleep on my return to the chalet.

It's such a luxury to put on fresh clothes every morning. Enjoyable, like an intense physical pleasure. Even to drop the dirty washing into the laundry bag is a real thrill. It's new freedom from the degrading scrutiny and scolding and punishments I'd known in former households and homes. Here the laundry all goes together, anonymously, to be washed and then returned in small piles from which we pluck our own garments and place them neatly in tidy drawers. Out of these, like magic, we appear, clad in our perfect, snow-white, long-sleeved cotton vests and panties.

The bothering discharge I had suffered from in England is being treated. Penicillin, Terramycin and any amount of other 'cin' wanders up me.

I was good on skis now, and today I had been chosen to race in the school team.

On this day also I had been invited to Paris by Magda. As I pulled out my fresh vest and pants, I sang, 'Oh, what a beautiful morning, oh, what a beautiful day,' and Magda chirped in with 'I 'ave a vonderful veelin', hevery sing goes it my fey!'

We had begun to practise the piano together. I was learning to accompany a girl playing Mozart's flute concerto. Ivo played the flute too and came up to play with us one night. The condensed water at the end of his flute started to dribble down the back of my neck. All the girls came up to tease me later, telling me not to wash my neck any more! I felt uneasy.

In the hut, the joy was slowly going out of the kissing. It began to develop into a strange game. Ivo wanted to take over my body. As with Father, I didn't understand why I should do things that I hated with my body. Ivo got annoyed if I didn't want to participate. Why did I have to put up a bashful pretence of coy excuses, to try and hug to myself what he wanted to take over? It began to feel rotten. I'd rather have been with the girls. I grew more and more depressed and didn't want to go to the hut, but felt I had to.

Then one night it happened.

I don't remember how. All I remember is that his kisses were good again and that I was tired of fighting him. I had no right to, I was stupid and a prude. He wanted and needed a woman. If I wanted this glorious man, I had to be that woman. So I just surrendered to his searching hands. I didn't know what was right or wrong. He was my teacher. The worst inhibition we had to overcome was my fear of not being freshly washed – I mean one hour ago, not five seconds before. I had a phobia about cleanliness and smells. I wondered, again and again, why God had made us smell like we did. Body odour! Why had He made it? Couldn't it be sweet smelling, like roses?

Ivo was saying, 'I love you, my darling. I long for you day and night and never get tired of looking at you.'

I pushed a piece of chocolate in his mouth. I was hungry.

'Among all those girls you stand out like a sun. You shine with such beauty.' He brushed gentle kisses all over my nose, my cheeks, my neck and mouth, so gently, oh, so tenderly, while all the time his hands were finding their way beneath the elastic band of my underpants. One finger was wedged slightly into my most secret little place. And despite the sudden flash of memory, and Father's face, with his nasty eyes, I listened to these other feelings with all my senses. What was this delightful new sensation? The swelling, the overtaking, the gorgeous explosion? I yelled out with the splendour. I hardly knew when it was over because the magic lasted forever.

After a long time he lifted his face to me. It was a new face. All I could breathe was, 'Wow! Wow! Wow!'

He smiled. He said, 'Wow! Wow! My sweety. I am proud.

We stayed close together for a long time, and then I asked, 'And you?'

'I have time, my sweety. We'll get rid of the old fears and skeletons first. We have time.'

At the mention of the word skeleton, I saw Father again, bony and skinny, saying, 'I want you to come. You must. Hurry. Now! Now! Now!' I hadn't been able to feel anything but his rough thumb. In time I had learned to pretend so that he would let me go, but first he'd jump away and grab my hand, clasping it round himself, saying, 'Now me!'

As Ivo started to get up, I clung to his hand in terror. Now, with one blow, it would all become terribly ordinary and awful.

'In our thoughts we're always together. When we're married we'll cuddle up together. We'll make such beautiful love, you'll never get enough. I bet you'd like to repeat all this now, if we could?'

As if he was hypnotising me, a surge of fierce longing struck me. I didn't realise then how deeply dependent on him he had made me, that night.

In time I began to resent Ivo. I wished it had never started. I wanted to be one of the girls. Why was I always the odd one out? Why did I have to be sure people took special notice of me? Liked me? And then once I was sure, why did I resent everything?

I didn't have the courage not to go to the hut, once or twice a week, but I began to be the fly on the ceiling again. As with Father, I pretended it wasn't happening to me. I wasn't really there. I had learned, a long time ago, to function mechanically. I was trained to please. This was supposed to be my future – my safety, my love, lover, fiancé, husband!

Already I was hating it. Was Father right in saying I was abnormal?

I wondered if it had to do with Mother often sending me away? Was that why I had to prove all the time that I was worth taking special notice of? Worth loving? Worth taking seriously? Why couldn't I just sit there in class like the others? Why did I feel so awfully inferior unless somebody made a fuss of me! How I longed to be just one of the giggling crowd. Now, I didn't feel at home here nor there. Why? Life was one big contradiction. When I was with my own group, I felt different and left out – not speaking the same language. I hated and envied them for their unconcern. They were so much luckier. Here, with Ivo, I felt things expected of me that I didn't know how to handle.

One night, I just knew I couldn't stand it any more.

The school had gone to a ball. Somehow we were alone. He took me to the cellar, to the ironing-room, where there were no windows. He laid me on the ironing table, underneath the bare bulb. He wanted to explore me, to see me and to look. He exposed himself, out of his zip, and it looked as ugly as Father's. I felt sick again.

That same night I wrote to Mother, in desperation. It was all becoming too much, the hiding, the secrets, the estrangement from the girls and other teachers. I wanted to go away for a time. I needed a rest. I wrote that I missed her and Andreas and wanted to see them, see the new house they were building, and the dog.

I met them one week later, at the train station in Basel. Ivo had waved goodbye to me, in Gstaad, with a look that to me seemed to say, 'Traitor'. I cried for half of my trip, which spoilt the journey.

It is a beautiful part of my country, the Bernese Oberland. The farmhouses have roofs reaching nearly to the ground, and from the train I watched the toy-like fences dance past, like toy soldiers with miniature bayonets, guarding squares of brown soil in the midst of the green meadows. These were dotted with sunflowers, cabbages and carrots, and sometimes shaded by manure heaps, compost, as neat as everything else in Switzerland. The cows, the bells, the rolling pastures, all framed by mountains which gleamed in the distance, then the lake. Boats bobbing, a few yachts with white sails billowing, children waving as our neat train chuffed by.

I read *Werther's Suffering* by Goethe and cried some more, strangely comforted at the expense of some fellow sufferer. I submerged myself in this grief.

Then we met, at the station. Rex, sniffing my hand, didn't find me worthy of a wag of his tail, but Mother and Andreas seemed pleased to see me. They congratulated me on my fluent French, called me 'such a grown-up young lady'. Mummy thought I didn't look well, and rather tired.

They still lived in the apartment next to the surgery for half the week.

On our second day they took me to see the new house. As I was totally unprepared for what I saw, I fainted. It must have been the rush of emotions on seeing the most beautiful house I had ever set eyes on — and knowing, deep down, that it was never for me. I felt swept in and thrown out as if in a gust of a wild, bleak gale. When I came to, they were very upset and helpful. Andreas was a wonderful doctor and soothingly concerned.

Mother's house looked like an English cottage, with honeysuckle by the door. Inside it had half walls upholding glass showcases full of her special treasures and Andreas's antique and valuable Egyptian collection. Queen Anne and Louis Philippe had been added to Mother's other beautiful furniture. Everywhere I looked, I sensed value, beauty and taste in the exquisite items ornamenting this home.

The bedrooms were decorated with chintz. Walls, curtains, lamps, bedspreads, picture frames and mirror frames all matching. And one of the rooms was for me!

The bathroom was of black tiles. Mother had painted red, exotic fish, aquarium-like, on the walls. It looked *très chic*.

I adored the whole place. The hearts in the shutters were cut according to my wish!

The weeks passed all too quicky, with many a lovely evening and lots of laughs in our new home, or eating out in the Alsace across the French border where they invited me for chicken and chips and lettuce with garlic. We had wonderful hours together.

I loved these two who had such a special love between them. They'd met over a septic thumb I had when I was two, just before my father went to live and work in Bradford. As Andreas was a well-known surgeon in Basel, it had been very difficult for him to get a divorce, and living together was frowned upon. He was a soft person, but a dear one. So was Mother. (I felt more grown-up to call her that, now. She didn't like it, though.)

I could not but notice that Mother was beginning to develop a phobia about cleanliness and tidiness in her new house. I couldn't leave a book and go to the loo but she'd have everything straightened up. We couldn't leave a drop in the handbasin, or a crumb on the kitchen chrome bench, or a towel, damp, in the bathroom. We laughed and teased her, but she got mad and didn't speak to me for hours.

At times she used to explode into a real rage over items of clothing or other belongings of mine. She would suddenly fuss, clean and scrub and tidy, non-stop, muttering under her breath. I felt it was my fault. She used to have daily help, and Frau Dresden in Bradford. Now, she couldn't bear a blemish on her home. It developed into such a mania that laughing didn't help. I felt I was in her way, or the cause of the dirt and dust. What hurt most was that I had the impression she hated having to do anything for me. I was going soon, and tried to talk to her, but I found her a different person, at times almost a stranger. Could a house do this? Or did it have anything to do with Father's suicide and why he'd done it? Or the divorce that wasn't coming through? I mostly blamed myself, and had fallen back into this 'guilt blame thing' which undermined all my newly found self-confidence. The old familiar heavy feeling was back, on my chest, squashing and burdening me.

I wanted to look forward to seeing Ivo again, but couldn't. What was wrong with me?

He was at the station, tanned, tall and blond, flicking his hair off his forehead. Smiling, he helped me off the train.

He was all I had.

Chapter Ten

And, on top of a mountain, he told me! On top of Mount Eggli, he tried to put it into words, all the way up in the wind on the chairlift, our skis dangling on cold feet.

'For a long time, I have wanted to tell you, but there was no point until now. I was married, before, in Amsterdam. Catholic. I left seven years ago, at the age of twenty-five, but it's hard to get a divorce. I'll try, darling, I'll try now, because I would like to marry you when you're eighteen.'

There it was – my first love affair! Not a romantic movie, but a sad one. What was I to say? Say, with a numb, bleeding 'something' inside. Everywhere around us, girls and ski instructors stood. Shivering. It was a horrible day. Hostile eyes observing. Not to let the pain thaw, not to think, I stood on my skis and flew straight down the mountain, one schuss, in a straight line. I gathered speed, fell and broke my leg.

I lay still and alone. An eternity in hell. I didn't ever want to go there.

Later he wrote me a poem. Later he came to see me in hospital. The poem was beautiful, but something more than my leg was broken.

I took weeks to feel better.

I was fifteen.

When I used to feel low like this, in England, I'd run up to the Yorkshire moors. It had been the only thing that helped. Here, I decided, I'd take my books and homework to the top of a mountain. I'd sit somewhere, alone, surrounded only by beauty and the sun and silence.

As I limped along the country lanes, the weight began to lift. I sucked in the fresh air and feasted my eyes upon the splendid, majestical giants with their sun-gleaming iced peaks, treed boundaries, dotted chalets and wooden stables. The stillness and freshness surrounded me. To hell with problems, I told myself. I'd had nothing but problems ever since I could remember. I wanted to live one day without that heavy weight on my chest.

'Please God, whoever you are and if you are, please take away this pressure. I'm sick and tired of it, and it's always there as if I need to feel ashamed when I'm happy.' I sat on the chairlift. It felt delightfully independent to do something all alone. At the top I wandered across to a lone stable with a platform full of hay laid out to catch the sun. The wooden wall was hot through my pullover and smelled of baking. The perfume of the hay mingled strongly. I flopped against the warmth, closed my eyes and felt the sun caress my face. I began to feel good all over. After about thirty minutes, I half-heartedly opened my history book. What a lot of dates to cram into my mind when I hadn't even worked out the ones in my own life! Once I'd written a similar sort of list in my diary. I turned to those pages.

1936 My birth.
1935 Have a mother and a father and we live in Basel.
Annemarie is the first girl they have for me. Later Nanny.
1938 In this year Mummy and Daddy go to look for a house
in Bradford. Mummy met Andreas because of my septic
thumb. Later I'm told many confusing different things.
(a) that Mummy and Daddy went to England and I stayed
with Nanny in Basel. (b) That Nanny then crossed the
channel with me, that Mummy then left us all there and
went back to Basel, came back, only to return to
Switzerland with me and Nanny because the war broke
1939 out. Daddy stays in England all through the war.
Apparently Nanny had a crush on my father. All I
remember is that we had a sandpit in the garden and I
had bright red and blue trousers which I loved. When
we came back to Basel, I had to go and live in Rapperswil
near Zürich, with Nanny's parents, because it was safer
there. I wondered why Mummy lived in the unsafe part
and I was worried about her. What if they dropped a
bomb on her? I also prayed every night that the Germans
wouldn't drop a bomb on Daddy's head in England. I
prayed for him but couldn't remember him.
1940 Rapperswil. I love it there. Have a real Grossmutter and
1941 Grossvater. They are wonderful and love me.
Mummy and I go to the Italian part of Switzerland, the
Tessin, for almost a year. We live in a pension where a
nice lady looks after me and I go to kindergarten and can

soon speak Italian. One day a man in the street wants to buy me chocolate and to take me home. I have on a short light blue dress. I thank him politely, tell him that my Mummy does not allow me to go home with strangers but if he wants to bring me chocolate home to our pension, he is most welcome to. He doesn't. Mummy is locked out one whole cold night. I'm frightened and Mummy catches meningitis.

1943 Mum and I often listen to music and I have to guess between Mozart, Beethoven, Bach, Brahms and Tchaikovsky, or we sing songs out of operas and have to guess. Peter comes to our place with his sister, Veronica. We play 'wedding'. Mummy dresses us up. She is the parson and takes us up and down in the lift, which is our honeymoon. Peter insists that we both prick our fingers with a needle, press our blood together, to be blood-related for ever and ever. Mum takes us out for tea and cakes, to the Huguenin, a Viennese-style café. She takes us to the toy department in Knopf and buys us a ball and glass marbles. We have many lovely times there, since we live in the new flat.

1943 I'm seven! First day of school. Have my first best friend Yvette! She is very beautiful and looks Italian. We get a puppy! Michael. A mongrel, all white with huge black blotch over left eye. There were two children's homes and different families before the next one. They were not too bad. Don't know the years or how long I was there for.

1944 F'burg. The most awful children's home, where we had to stand in rows and show our underpants and got punished for the slightest mark. Where I was forced to eat so strictly and cruelly that I couldn't eat with strangers for years. Where we were sent to church with plasters across our mouths.

1945 Back with Mummy and dog. Back to Gotthelf school with Yvette. One day we fight, one day we make up, because of the new friends she's made, till I meet Heidi Haas, who is another good friend, the cleverest one in the class. She told us about Hitler and the Jews and the concentration camps. Everybody was talking about it. I could hear Mummy and her friends and Andreas talk in hushed, frightened voices, as I tried to fall asleep. And in my mind I'd think up what one could write or say to Hitler to make him stop frightening the whole world.

1945 The war ends! Many GI's walk around Basel and we all
1946 learn to say 'Chewing-gum, please'. They laugh and give generously. They look great in their uniforms. They have

helped to get rid of Hitler. England has won! We hear about Churchill's speeches. He is a very wonderful, strong, good leader. What a good thing there are such men.

Peter takes me to the theatre. To Mozart's *Magic Flute*. Sarastro. What a low voice! Queen of the Night. What a Soprano! What melodies! What beauty! Oh, I loved it. Peter said he'd looked at me from the side, all through it and that I looked 'Christmas-tree happy'. He held my hand and I felt a bit embarrassed. But it was all so wonderful, I sing the songs all day and when I roll and fall asleep.

1947 Father comes. Wants to take us back to England. I can't remember him. Mummy and Andreas are sad. We go to Bradford. A black city. A black house. A German housekeeper. I was often a bad girl in Basel, but I never knew I was so bad. Father is always having to punish and hurt me. Somewhere about this time he starts coming to my bed. Piano lessons! Nightmares! The ghosts! Meet two boys at school that speak German and meet their parents, the Rosenbergs. We all become friends but the boys play more with boys.

1948 Still the same. Dreary, awful, frightening life. Mummy is scared of Father, so is Frau Dresden. The best part are Chappy and Glenny, our two dogs. Mum becomes famous. She goes to an art club, exhibits and is even in the newspaper with photos of her pictures. She did one of the Bradford town hall with all the electric poles and wires, in front. It's black and white charcoal. Very good. She does flowers in vases with brass candlesticks, in oil, all with the highlights and shadows. Marvellous. I don't know how she does it. She catches the sad Brontë atmopshere of the moors. I adore her pictures. She paints the nights through, as then no one disturbs her and she says she forgets how homesick she is. Uncle Percy is a dales painter. He's a new friend, banker, painter, actor. He takes us to the civic playhouse and we all see a funny play. We have a big party on New Year's Eve and Swiss people from the firm come and friends from the arts club and we all play games. Uncle Percy does a few sketches, acts the 'lady in the bath'. We all laugh and have a wonderful time and I'm amazed it can be like this and sorry it can't always be. Sweets are still rationed. I meet Miss Abbott. Had nits from the children in school that live in slums.

1950 Gets worse and worse. Have no friends. Can't join in with

Guide camp or parties. Father won't let me. I can hardly bear to live. Would rather die. Miss Mummy and her love. She's off to Basel every so often. Frau Dresden is kinder to me when Mummy's gone. She lets me listen to 'Mrs Dale's Diary' after school, and makes puddings, and if Father is not home I can listen to 'Dick Barton, Special Agent', and 'The Tommy Handley Show' and Wilfred Pickles in 'Have a go, Jo!' I can laugh and forget everything then and it's so cosy, but it's not the same as Mummy. Once I was allowed to go to a party, when Mummy was back. I play 'Postman's Knock' and 'Hyde Park Corner' and 'Adams Staircase' where there is a lot of 'lights out' and a grab and a kiss. I got kissed for the very first time and felt ever so proud. David was his name and he was tall and 15 and walked me home and stopped to kiss me again in an alley. I came in as if on a cloud and said, 'I've been kissed. Isn't a kiss a wonderful thing?' The next day Father came up to me and told me that the lady who had given the party had rung up and had said that I'd behaved dreadfully and had opened one of the boys' flies. I was so shocked, I began to cry. It was my first, lovely party and now Daddy was spoiling it again and it was all lies. Why did these things always happen to me? He told me he wouldn't pursue the matter, wouldn't go to the lady, and I must tell no one but that it was the last party I'd been to. I couldn't understand the lady and why she should tell my father such a lie. I couldn't eat, felt ashamed, couldn't sleep and finally did nothing but cry. I got shingles on my back, which itched maddeningly and had to have the doctor. Whenever he came, such a kind man, I felt like crying. He said it was very unusual for a child of my age to have such migraines and shingles. The next day I cried. Mummy asked me what was the matter and I told her how I couldn't understand what this lady had told Father. Mummy immediately rung her up and was told that I had behaved perfectly at the party and had been helpful and polite. We both couldn't understand it.

1951 Daddy had to go to Ishcia for his arthritis. I like life without him much better. I see a lot of Miss Abbott, play with Pat, next door, and go to Girl Guides and have Fish and Chips after. I'm invited to birthday parties and Mummy takes me to see grown-up pictures. I love Elizabeth Taylor best and Gregory Peck, James Mason and Anne Todd in the *Seventh Veil,* adore Jimmy Stewart and June Alison, Judy Garland and Fred Astaire in *Easter*

Parade, Danny Kaye, *Rhapsody in Blue*, love Gershwin instantly. I see Anouk in the *Golden Salamander*, and Charles Boyer in *Gaslight* which makes me think of my father, and get over-excited in *The Third Man* with Orson Welles. What actors and stories! I'm always one of the stars when I come out, and I live the part for days! Must be 'luvely' to be a star with everybody loving you!
I told! Father came back. He shot himself. Miss Killarney came. Both our Swiss friends from the firm, who went to get the police, were instantly sacked. Lost their jobs. They should have first gone to the boss. I'm unlucky for everybody.

1952 To Basel with Aunty Elly Zimmerman. Tennis! Mummy!

1952 She arrives without Glenny. Andreas! Rex! Me off to the chalet school at Gstaad.

The sun blazed hot on top of my head, yet I felt cold and stiff at the bottom of my back. I padded it with hay and sat more comfortably. What a child I'd been! What a stupid goody-goody. Nearly as dumb as Pollyanna. But I still didn't dare to be much different today. The way I'd written this. It did give me a good summary. What a strange life! Not one I'd like my child to have.

I decided to continue this list at some stage, later. I was behind in my diary and decided to catch up now.

1952 We're into psychology now. Read Jung and Freud and books by American psychoanalysts. I read of things called 'complexes', 'worry', 'stress', 'anxiety', 'fear', 'phobia', 'trauma' and 'neuroses'. Funny things. I decide never to have any of them. It's only for hysterical females, as Daddy and Mummy would say.
Ivo wants to become a writer. He looks interesting, sitting in a corner of the room, writing, with his pipe, blowing out smoke in that special way when he is pensive. I'd like to become a writer. It's fabulous to sit there, pen in hand, clean new page, and just wait, to be surprised with the wisdom that 'poureth forth'! If it comes, that is. Mostly it's just dumb and frustrating, making me feel foolish, certain that I had *les follies des grandeurs*. After a writer, I'd like to be an actress. Or help with crippled children – I don't know. Mummy said, 'You'd have to be a different person for an actress.' I suppose she was right. Who was I to opt for such a wonder? She also said, 'It's just wanting to show off . . . there is a lot of the

exhibitionist in you . . . always speaking out of turn, interrupting people, when they talk . . . saying things to attract attention to yourself. You'll have to learn an awful lot, first.'

I'd asked what she meant. She said that it was being narcissistic. That it came from Narcissus, a Greek boy who always looked at himself in a pond, as they didn't have mirrors in those days. He was in love with himself. Funny, the parson at school had said you had to love yourself, before you could love anyone else properly. The world of grown-ups seems full of strange contradictions. In our psychology classes Ivo played games called, 'free-associations'. It brought back strange memories. Ivo said he wondered whether my mother and father had bought a book called, 'How to make my child have total lack of self-confidence, the biggest inferiority complex possible and have guilt feelings all the time'.

The sun was lower now. I felt suddenly cold. It was time to get back. I'd learn my history in bed. My chairlift carried me down slowly, clanking at each pillar, through such unspoilt beauty that it was not possible to feel anything but good.

It was lovely to get back into the hum-drum of girls' chatter, music and clatter, as the tea and huge loaves of bread, butter and jam were being prepared, in the cosy small lounge where the open log fire crackled and spat at this time of the day.

The weeks sped by. Magda, Sally, a lovely girl from Scotland, and I, were into knitting. With the thickest needles, we knitted pullovers, scarves and caps for everybody in sight. Whether we were sunbathing on balconies or propped up in beds, or sprawling all over the comfy nooks and crannies of the chalet, our needles could be heard clicking in time to the evergreens we sang. Magda was now good looking in a studious sort of way, and Sally was simply stunningly pretty. She had long blond hair, which she twirled high on top of her head, accentuating her slender long neck.

She loved acting and was always role playing, shouting up to us from beneath a balcony, 'Juliet! My Juliet! Romeo! Where art thou now, my Romeo?' Or she'd pretend not to be able to say her Rs or her Ls and be from Germany, and suddenly reciting, 'Go to ze nunnewy, Ophenia!' She would rush to a mirror, squeezing out an imaginary blackhead with great to-do, shouting, 'Out, out, black spot!' And while we were out walking, she'd suddenly come racing up to us, arms out, shouting, 'Heathcliff! Heathcliff!' Then mime a sort of Hollywood happy-ending embrace. We had a time of laughter and schoolgirlish giggling. Only my unshared secret about Ivo made me feel disloyal at times.

And then the great day arrived! The day on which nineteen girls, Patsy, Madame, Ivo and I went to Paris, via Basel, on the night-train. Paris! We sang and ate and talked all night. I don't know what sort of a special place I'd imagined – made of gold, or marble or coloured pavements, I don't know – but the first impression was grimy and ordinary. Just like any other big city with tired, poorly dressed people going to work. I did see some well-dressed ladies but the main attraction, the one that the French girls got excited about, anyway, was that most people were carrying long thin breads called 'flutes'.

Magda and I were met by her parents; the others went to a hotel. Monsieur and Madame de B. were aristocrats from the village de B., owned and lived in the Castle de B. – a very noble family. I thought they were a good-looking, awe-inspiring couple, as they embraced Magda briskly and greeted me. When in Paris, they lived in an imposing looking house in the best *arrondissement*, to which we now drove through the most confusing, mad traffic I had ever seen, with taxi-drivers yelling '*Imbécile*!' or continually pointing one finger at their head as if to shoot themselves. I was laughingly informed that this gesture insinuated 'idiot!'.

Magda's parents had servants like I didn't know were still of this world. A *livrée* with white gloves pulled back my chair at the dinner table, and I was astounded to experience how quickly I could get used to such noble treatment. I found it fun to adapt to this aristoratic new way of life, rather like one learns a part in a play. As I automatically sat and spoke and walked and ate differently, I imagined with delight that this was how a chameleon must feel as it adapts its colour. I could only now understand why Magda had been so thrilled, at school, to make her own bed or tidy away her own things. Here, I was surprised we were permitted to clean our own teeth, everything was so refined and quietly, invisibly done for us.

We girls had quarters of our own, at the bottom of a spiral staircase in a spacious, light part of the house. Five rooms: a children's library, crammed with classical books, books to provide every kind of knowledge, and rows of books with photographs on any subject in the world. There was a whole section on art and music. Then there was a playroom full of antique rocking-horses bought from old roundabouts at fairs, porcelain dolls, dollshouses with real electric lights, furnished intricately, exquisite toys, modern remote-controlled cars and planes . . . I could have stayed there forever.

There was a huge pink marble bathroom with mirrors on the ceiling and on all the walls and two bedrooms as large as a whole apartment. And what beautiful clothes and shoes Magda had! Yet she hated everything about her home and her family. All she dreamed of was the simple life, a cottage in the country, with her piano, and a man to love. It was a vague dream and she was often in a trance-like daydream. When I managed to tease her out of one, she'd become amazingly lively, would laugh and cry, becoming hilarious to a point of near hysteria. Her parents called her unbalanced. They would either confront and shower us with an unnatural amount of attention, to a point of exaggeration that made me uncomfortable, or would ignore us altogether. Then Magda and I would sit straight, hands in laps, eyes demurely cast down, until their loud exclamations, 'Ah! *Mais que les demoiselles sont adorables!*' had us performing once more, like monkeys sitting up for applause and a tit-bit. It was all unreal.

Paris! The twenty of us trooped through the Louvre. Dutifully we oohed and ahhed in front of 'Mona Lisa', Renoirs, Manets, and Lautrecs, proving to our supervisors and to ourselves how very cultured we were, while surreptitiously stifling yawns. Versailles. How beautiful! Les Invalides. Who was interested where Napoleon's old kidneys, liver and heart lay?

The Eiffel Tower was more fun. At last, there from the top, I suddenly understood why everybody got so excited about Paris. There it lay, like a huge star, boulevards going off in all directions, one of them the famous Champs Elysées. And I could see L'Arc de Triomphe, la Place de la Concorde, Notre Dame, the Seine, Sacré Coeur and Les Bois. Then, down from the tower there were all the shops and the fashion, the bistros and boulevard cafés. What fun to sit and watch people, especially the men and boys, turn and smile at us, twenty young ladies *'de l'Engleterre'*.

I'd almost forgotten about Ivo. I mean, about him not just

being a teacher to me as to the others. I wanted so much to be one of the girls, to be submerged in the fun of this exciting time, just carefree. After three days he ignored me and sulked. The old lead weight began to creep back on to my chest. He got me aside in a restaurant while everyone was choosing cake. 'One would think I didn't exist, for you,' he snapped. 'Is this what the Paris trip means to you? To forget and ignore me? You must feel a lot for me.'

'Ivo. Don't be like this. It's all so complicated, what with me staying at Magda's and she having such a crush on you. She and her mother talk about nothing else but you and it's embarrassing enough. I feel awful. Why can't we just have a fun, normal time, like everybody else? Just girls and teachers?'

'Ah! Those snobs mean more to you than I do, do they? And to be accepted by them is more important, to you, is it?'

'Ivo! Please don't. This hurts and it's not fair. You're not being logical. I'm invited by them, Magda's my friend and we're here as a group from the institute, so we do have to behave and be careful. Don't make it harder for me than it already is. You know I love you and want to be with you.' (But it's great to get away from you, too, and just be me, I added to myself.)

'Well, let's do something about it then. I'll make some excuse and see if we can manage a day to ourselves. Leave it to me.' He walked away. I slunk back to my table and said I didn't want any cake. Why had he made the light switch off in Paris? Why wasn't I pleased because he loved me so much and missed me?

'You look furious. What's the matter?' Magda asked, as she'd seen us talking. 'He always seems to single you out. I mean, at school it was because of your French and yoga and maths, but why here?'

'He always seems to find some fault. I don't know. I hate teachers.' I felt ashamed for both.

The next day Magda's mother came to our room to announce that she'd had a phone call from a teacher, Patsy O'Neill, and that a taxi would call for me, to take me to Madame Baumont, as she'd been instructed by my mother to buy some French things.

The taxi took me to a small, back-street hotel.

Ivo stood behind the glass entrance-door. He looked so boyishly pleased that I told my sinking heart to stop plummeting. He whisked me off into some clanky metal elevator and then into a small bedroom with a bidet.

'How did I do that? Eh? Come to me, my darling. I'm so sorry I was nasty yesterday. I love you so. I missed you.' He gathered me up in a strong embrace. It felt good to be close to him. A blackbird was singing a solitary song somewhere outside and I closed my eyes so as not to see the dingy room. It made me feel cheap, like the prostitutes we had seen on the Paris pavements. He said, 'You look lovely. It's so cruel not to be able to openly put my arm around you.'

'It's a strain, all along.'

He sat down on the bed and pulled me onto his lap. I had on some of Magda's lovely high heels and one of her best *tailleurs*. I felt very smart for him. He said, 'Why don't you get out of that ridiculous attire and cuddle up to me? It makes you look like a little girl trying to dress up like her mother.' He laughed. 'We have four hours.'

Indignantly I said, 'Don't you like this? I think it's so beautiful. You are horrible.'

'First of all, I will never be able to afford such fashion trash, so don't you start getting infected by those snobbish ideas. Second, I love my simple, natural little girl. No fancy stupid rags, made expensive by a Dior or some-such nametag, which is all a load of baloney anyway. And thirdly, you don't need clothes. You look best without them.'

I felt let down.

'I've been longing to wander through town, hand in hand with you. Can't we go and see a film or shop or drink something, just the two of us? Surely Paris is big enough? It would be so lovely, just the two of us, freely and alone.'

'What about cuddling up together, freely and alone?'

I knew it would have been normal for me to want this as much as him, but I felt flat, not in the mood. Why was this sex business often so unpleasant to me? It was all the girls ever talked and dreamed about.

'What's so good about walking around streets or sitting in cafés or films if at last we can be really close and together, undisturbed?'

What was wrong with me? I was hurting his feelings. I made myself smile coquettishly as I dropped my skirt, took off my jacket, lost my shoes and sat down on the bed beside him in my dainty petticoat. He pecked my cheek with an appreciative sound and walked over to the basin, rolling his eyes in fun-approval. I tried to match his mood with mine, blushing. He soon came back and I saw his whole beautiful muscular body for the first time. He clambered on to the bed behind me and scrambled under the covers. He still had on his underpants. I sat there stiffly.

'Aren't you cold?'

'My feet are cold.'

'Well, how about that! Let's warm those poor little feet then.' He leaned over to feel. He gathered me to him and bundled me under the covers. I snuggled close and then didn't dare to move. I thought, here I lie again, against my will, again not doing what I want to do. Why is what I want to do never important enough to do? It was such fun yesterday, in Paris. Such harmless, free fun. I felt a nasty, strangling feeling gather inside my throat, irking me into wanting to scream and kick and yell, 'I don't want! I don't want! I don't know what and why, but I don't want!' But the thought was stupid and immature and hurtful. I had no right but to comply.

I felt him stiff up against me – and it was Father! Whenever I'd hoped just to cuddle and get warmth, the 'threat' had begun to jump in muscular spasms. Up against me, lifting its ugly head against me, ready to want to tear me apart and rub me sore. Oh, how I hated that part and how hard it was to accept this as part of the parcel, to get the warmth and closeness in the end.

Here goes, I thought, and closed my eyes as I had done so many miserable times before. And as he began to get what he wanted and liked, I escaped out of my body, through my mind. I was with the girls, in the shops, in a film, buying beautiful things, pretty trinkets, riding in the *Bois de Boulogne* in superbly tailored clothes – living and loving, without sex. All the time I mechanically made the right sounds, responses, movements and touches. But it was not me.

I took a taxi home to Magda's sitting as on eggs, sore. I was glad I'd be leaving Gstaad soon. I'd miss the mountains, the scenery and the beauty of the old chalet, miss my cherished, serene, Heidi surroundings. I'd miss the school and the memories of falling in love. My excited breathlessness when he suddenly appeared; the thrill of hearing his voice. The silent, secret look of love, knowing that out of all the others, he loved me, that I was worth loving most. But now his nearness had become too near and I couldn't cope, was suffocating. I wanted him, missed him, but was not ready, not yet. When would I be? Would I ever be normal? Or was I mad, or cold?

Two days later we all left Paris to return to school. The night before we'd all gone out to a cabaret called 'Lapin Agile'. Here the artists sang songs and everyone clapped their hands together in a certain rhythm sequence. Magda got tipsy and kept shouting, '*Egalité, egalité!* I'd like a simple life! It's in my mind, it's in my mind and never works in *realité! Realité!*' She looked slightly mad as she clapped and chanted this all evening, crying and laughing because we were to leave Paris the next day.

We returned to the mountains.

I caught Ivo's eye and smiled whenever I could. The train sang, 'I love you and I'll miss you, but I need to get away. I love you and I'll miss you but I need to get away.' Before I fell asleep in my corner seat (against his coat which hung above me and smelled deliciously of him), tears welled up. I was tired and completely mixed up.

Paris was over and with it my first night at a Paris theatre. I had looked forward madly to this occasion but it had passed, leaving no special impression, because over all was Ivo with his demands and expectations, covering everything else as with a heavy cloak. Everybody had been raving about the play, *Le dialogue des Carmelites*. I had only realised, with horror, how little I knew and how much history I had to catch up on.

School had me back for one more week. A sad one, and then I slept in Gstaad for the last time.

Chapter Eleven

L'Ecole de Commerce in Neuchâtel is world famous. Mother took me by train. Trains reminded me of Gross-papa in Zürich and the happiest year of my life I had spent there. The memory still hurt so I pushed it away.

'Neuchâtel,' Mother said, and I saw the lake, the small town, the imposing castle and its old town wall.

'Looks lovely,' I said lamely, still afraid of change.

We walked down the wide road that led to the town and lake, then up the hill to the castle, and along to where my new dwelling-place stood in the Rue Jeanne de Hochberg. The house looked high and stern, as did the two ancient mademoiselles who were to look after me – very Prussian, wrapped in long black robes, frills at their withered throats held there by black velvet bands, keeping the loose skin together, to make them look less turkey-like. One, I saw instantly, was wearing a wig. *Une perque!* How funny! What if we were to see her without! They welcomed us and led us into their parlour, which was draped in heavy velvet curtains and crowded with massive dark green plush furniture. I sat primly, desperate to make a good impression under Mummy's stern glance. We were ushered to my bedroom, which was dark, high, and hollow-sounding.

After explaining that I had a fiancé who was older and responsible, and permitted to come and see me every third weekend, my mother left. We kissed and she squeezed me hard. I sat in my room – sat there from five till seven. An eternity!

A bell summoned me to the dining room. There I saw two more old women, one even older man and six girls of my own age. One girl was stocky, with a cheeky grin, two were extremely pretty, the rest uninteresting. We sat down. Mademoiselle Clara served the soup, Mademoiselle Agathe served the next course, and after a short dispute on who had served the dessert the previous night, Mademoiselle Clara decided to serve. A fat, pimply-faced girl brought and cleared the food. She was doing her 'French-speaking household year'.

I didn't envy her, as we'd been instructed never to mix with the kitchen personnel.

The old man's teeth moved and clicked as he ate. The stocky girl caught my eye and glanced pointedly towards him, pretending to burst with laughter any minute. I looked away. Mademoiselle Clara introduced me to them all and I smiled. The grinning girl was called Violette. One of the women took a hairpin out of the back of her bun and stealthily poked her teeth. I looked at Violette and we both nearly burst. I had to pinch my thigh. The newness and silent chewing had a nerve-wracking effect on me.

After the meal, the girls invited me to see their rooms and we got acquainted. There was only one other new girl and Violette soon informed me that all the boys were after her and she'd been asked to leave her last pensione and was here on trial. She wore a dangerously low-cut blouse and Mademoiselle Clara asked her to the parlour. From then on she wore blouses up to her chin.

My new school was excellent and the teachers were good. It was a time of hard work. Shorthand-typing, commercial letters, book-keeping, all in French, was difficult. I found it dry and uninteresting, and was at a disadvantage anyway, because most of the students were sons and daughters of parents with big firms and businesses. They had more notion of what it was all about and where it was leading them in their future. To me it could just as well all have been Chinese. I was up many a night, trying to make my books balance, not finding the errors in the make-believe business I had to conduct. To me, business and figures, buying and selling, profit and losses, were unimaginative things that made no sense. I must have that part of the brain missing. I just learned off by heart like a parrot and after two years miraculously passed my diploma.

Our old chaperones were so strict that there were very few incidents out of that time worth relating.

Ivo came regularly. The nine boys and nine girls from my class respected me because of this fiancé figure. They watched us with envy as we walked hand in hand through the town and along the lake and into the favourite café, called Café Hemmler. It reminded us of Charlie's in Gstaad, except that we were here permitted the luxury of sitting close together. For a while this novelty heightened our mutual pleasure of being together. The day before his arrival I'd nearly go up the walls with joy and expectation. On Sunday night, an hour before his departure we would sit in our café saying we'd soon be wading knee-deep in our tears if we didn't pull ourselves together. It was romantic, and in the background the pianist played, *In einer kleinen Konditorei, da sassen wir zwei, bei Kuchen und The*. Afterwards I'd wave his train off and walk home, blinded by tears.

He was writing articles about philosophy, and as my work got harder and more demanding, I needed hours of extra coaching. When he came to visit, all he wanted to do was read me his tedious pages, which I couldn't understand. I couldn't concentrate and our times together became a strain. And as grateful as *I* was, he didn't like the fact that there was no possibility for sex. Our nearness and the thrill of touching and kissing was flickering low and slowly dying, like the flame on a burned-out candle. It only sparked a little on occasions.

But Ivo didn't come one visiting weekend, nor the next and he wrote to say that they had exams at the school and he was up to his ears in work. This had never happened before. It hurt. I reproached myself. Every day I rushed to the letterbox, but when his letters in his beautiful handwriting did arrive, they were filled with such difficult philosophical thoughts that I laid them aside. They were not love letters.

As he continued to stay away, and I began to miss him more than I'd ever realised I would, I decided to go to Gstaad to visit him for a surprise. I had enough pocket-money for the train fare. After a phone call to Mummy and one from her to the two mademoiselles, I was permitted to go.

On the trip back, I felt memories lurking behind every tree and bush, on every mountainside, inside houses and cafés. Everything I looked at seemed charged with emotions.

Near to tears, I walked up to school.

Here I had experienced the first talks about myself, and become aware of my fears, my likings and that there was such a thing as thirst for knowledge. The awareness for such things as love, spiritual things, classical literature and music and poetry had been awakened here. There had been insight into philosophies and psychology, even if only the mere beginnings. There had been the joys of the snow, the mountains, skiing, sledging, the night descents with wax and petroleum torches, with our ski instructors holding flares high beside us on the night pistes. Us singing and skiing after fondue parties in cosy huts on mountain tops.

I remembered the balls at the Palace Hotel where I'd been invited to dance by the Duke of Kent, to the disgust of the English girls, who were jealous and said a Swiss girl had no use for royalty! The village church where Yehudi Menuhin had played and had tea with us and talked about music like a friend. The 'Käserei', a chalet nightclub where I'd heard Elizabeth Taylor tease Richard Burton, and saw that her eyes were truly an amazing violet colour. Watching her checking her makeup in a small powder-box mirror, I'd wondered how anyone so famous and beautiful needed to worry about the way she looked! Where Bo-bo Rockefeller had invited me to dine at the Palace, because of a girl staying at our school, and I'd been in awe because everyone knew how much she'd received for her divorce. Millions! And I remember thinking that I'd rather not have a divorce, because even if I could buy everything I wanted, in all this world, money could never buy true love, could never buy a person that belonged to one, like my Ivo, to share a life, special togetherness and one's own children.

I thought of our first kisses in the hut. Ivo! Thought of my school friends who had become withdrawn and cool after Paris. Puzzles of the adult world, and me on its threshold.

My heart sang, now, as I could see the school chalet. I would see him, would surprise him. Would hold him and love him like never before. We could visit all our favourite places.

He was in his office, the door slightly ajar. He sat on a chair and at his feet, looking up at him with adoration, was a girl. Her face was turned up to him with a cigarette in her mouth and he was lighting it for her. The way he looked at her! In one short moment I knew all that there was to know. So that was why he had stopped coming and why his letters were lacking in that inexplicable quality.

As I stood there, watching them, I felt more ugly pain than I had ever felt before. Something made me take one step forward and push the door open. I just stood and stared. They didn't move.

He suddenly jumped up. 'What a surprise, Olivia! Where have you sprung from?'

There was electricity in the air.

'I've missed you, so I've come to see you.' I walked up to him and kissed him demonstratively on the mouth. He pulled back and I felt as if he'd hit me.

'Helene, this is Olivia. This is Helene.'

She looked unruffled. It annoyed me so much that I childishly blurted out, 'I've come to see how my fiancé is.' I knew that she could tell how I felt, and I was angry because she looked lovely.

'Where are you going to stay? Does Madame know you're here?' he asked.

'I think that is our concern, don't you? Surely you'll put me up in a hotel, as you've saved the expense of yours three times in a row in Neuchâtel? Here, we'll be free to see each other now, as I'm no longer a pupil of this school, in case you forgot.'

I sounded catty and was proud of it. I'd always felt too insecure to feel I had any rights. Anger seemed to help. Ivo looked stunned. He wasn't used to this tone.

Helene got up. 'I've got to get back to my boring class,' she said, and went. I sat down and hoped I wouldn't cry. I was beginning to shake all over.

'Have you found a new little girl, then?'

'We'll have to talk about it. I'm very fond of her, if that's what you mean, but I love you just as much. Nothing's changed.'

'That's a good joke. I'm sorry I can't believe you.'

'You will when we've talked. Anyway, why don't you go down to the village and book yourself into the Edelweiss and I'll meet you there for lunch after my last lesson.'

I got up to go. He tried to kiss my cheek, but I turned away and left.

I didn't see the mountains as I walked back, and suddenly I was in the hall of the hotel. Once in my room, I walked up and down, silent tears streaming down my face, changing into helpless, whimpering puppy sounds. By lunchtime I looked a perfect mess – could hardly see out of my eyes.

Downstairs, I waited in the farthest, darkest corner, ordering a tomato juice without looking up, rummaging in my handbag for dark sunglasses. How awful to look the way I did when competing with another girl. Why was he doing this to me? He who had insisted on being the first man in my life, he who had wanted to break me in. (What a way of putting it!) Had wanted to take my virginity. (That sounded even worse.) Why was he looking at that girl in that special way? God, I wanted him, now that I might lose him. I knew how desperately I loved and needed and wanted him. I felt my moonstone pendant at my throat and began to cry again.

He suddenly stood there.

I clung to my hanky, as if to save my life, and dabbed under my sunglasses and tried to get rid of the frog in my throat.

'If I love the sun, it doesn't mean that I can't love the moon,' he began, as he sat down besides me, putting his hand over mine. 'You know I love you, but I can be fond of other people too, can't I?'

'Very clever. I knew you'd come up with some explanation. You're so good at talking. Always were. You can do anything you like with us because you're older and wiser and more experienced. Gathering experience all the time, as I see! How do you think I felt when I saw you looking at another girl the way you did. I saw you.'

'Is it a crime if we like each other? Now that you've gone and I'm left with that bunch of spoilt brats, can you blame me for being pleased when a new one turns out to be nicer?'

'That's how it started with us, and she won't be able to help herself falling for you, but you're probably flattered. It must be just great to have all those lovely girls swooning all round you. You should know by now what an effect you have on women, so why the heck d'you have to prove it all the time? Anyone would think that it was you who has the inferiority complex!'

'*Touché!* So you're slaying me with my own weapons now!'

As he said this, I suddenly, instinctively, knew that crying would get me nowhere. All it did was make me look unattractive. *L'esprit*! Thoughts! These were the things that impressed this man. Whatever happened, I must try to show a brighter side. Must even pretend not to care.

I managed, out of some inner, hidden strength, to make a complete turnabout. I smiled at him.

'You're right, Ivo. After all, maybe there is a lot of advantage in all this. Helene is nice. I can't really blame her. Let's meet — the three of us — and talk it all over.'

'D'you really mean that? Why, that's wonderful! I knew I hadn't underestimated you. You are my very special little one, you know.'

Small electric shocks stung and twinged inside me, but I smiled.

I went to the toilet and dabbed lots of icy water on my face.

As I took deep breaths, I decided to fight this in a dignified way. Was this some inborn womanly wisdom or the Hollywood films I had seen?

I asked him to order wine.

After an hour I smuggled him up to my room and we made love like never before. Even I enjoyed it, with no pretence. Our tenderness and passion was fierce, sad and intensive, involving every fibre, our bodies like two instruments in perfect harmony. I had grown up a little. As we both climbed to a peak together, for the first time we were both crying, as if saying farewell forever.

'My darling. My darling. My darling!' Ivo sighed. 'You should always drink wine.'

The curtains were drawn. A tall wardrobe mirror reflected our bodies in the soft glow of a candle. 'I love that golden tone of your skin. It shines like copper. You are lucky to have such soft beautiful skin. I love every little part of you. What fabulous legs and breasts, such perfect proportions. I missed you so, my darling. Forgive me. Forgive me.'

We'd never been so close, so completely contented. I basked in every touch and every word.

For dinner, that same night, he brought Helene. She looked stunningly adult and lovely. Taller than me and more poised. Her self-assuredness nearly threw me for a second, but I concentrated on our 'love-in-the-afternoon'. Surely it meant just as much to him?

But the way he lit her cigarette shattered my confidence. It was enough to make me forget my repulsion of smoking. With what I thought was a very lady-like gesture, I drew one out of his packet and held it up. Looking slightly amused, Ivo raised his eyebrows and lit it. I could have kicked myself. Helene smoked on with the grace of the lady I yearned to be. I got smoke into the wrong place and had to cough. My eyes stung and watered. My tongue hurt, and as I tried to suppress the spluttering, it grew worse, never-ending. I managed to stub it out as if nothing had happened, talking on too quickly, feeling the perfect fool.

It didn't help to see Ivo trying to look unconcerned. The whole evening was a disaster, unnatural — and I was the loser.

'Let's go for a walk.'

In the moonlight we walked — Ivo in the middle. From Gstaad to Saanen, and from the village of Saanen back to

Gstaad, on and on, the whole night through.

'My mountains,' I silently cried, like a sentimental idiot, 'how sad to have to remember you like this, now.'

For as we talked, after a long silence, it did turn out that she loved him, really loved him. She was nineteen. I was sixteen. It seemed, too, that though he loved the sun and the moon, he loved her a little bit differently, and this is what nearly killed me, there and then, when he said, 'Helene has a broader pelvis. She looks more the mother type. Now don't misunderstand me, Olly. I love your mind, your thoughts, your wit, your deep wise understanding and eagerness to learn. I love your *esprit*, if you like [how that hit home!] but now I know what is missing. You don't look as if you'd be a mother of six, and Helene does. It's the motherliness that attracts me so irresistibly.'

I crumbled inside with the pain. I knew I had lost. I must not show how it hurt. I suddenly hated them both with such fury that I could barely control myself. He, who had built me up out of the deepest, lowest lack of self-esteem, had destroyed and crippled me more, in one instant, than anyone ever had done – or would.

We parted soon after those significant last words, and they thought they would see me the next day, but I crept into my room, where the bed was still crumpled, and I packed. Through the dawn I slunk to the tiny railway station in Gstaad, and there sat on a wooden bench to await the first train that would take me away.

Chapter Twelve

For me, nothing was ever the same after that, but life went on.

Basler Fasnacht! The Carnival of Basel!

I'd spent a wonderful family weekend in the new house. We'd all gone to bed early on Sunday, for at 3 o'clock in the morning we had to get up and go to the *Morgen-streich* (morning stroke) which begins at four. So far, all I'd known about this festival was that in Bradford, Mother used to get up at four in the morning each Fasnacht Monday to cook the traditional browned-flour soup and onion-and-cheese quiche, and howl her head off.

Now we stood among the waiting crowds lining the pavements of Basel. The moment was special. I wanted time to stand still. I felt so free and happy, with fun for three days and nights in front of me. I was seventeen. What was it going to be like?

The clock struck four. Every light in the city went out. Instantly from far and near, the drums and piccolos of all the huge carnival clubs, called 'cliques', began to beat out the *Morgen-streich*.

And then they came. From all sides. The lanterns, the pipes, the drums, the costumes, the masks, the huge figures of the drum majors, the headlamps and flashing funny lights on grotesque heads and huge wigs. Out of all the small and large side streets they came, drumming, piping, marching, blasting the magnificent sound into our hearts and stomachs shattering our eardrums. The sheer ecstasy of it, near unbearable, causing tears to roll, throats to contract and hearts to burst with joy. To me it was like nothing on earth.

As they passed, people fell in behind as the old tradition dictated. They mixed and squeezed and mingled, and me along with them. We all fell in behind a band, and slowly, slowly, step by step, to the fascinating beat of the old marches, followed as one slowly rocking mass – a whole people of a whole town united in an experience of tradition and beauty.

We had linked arms, Mother, Andreas and I. This must have

been one of the happiest moments in our lives together, yet.

And into this moment walked Tobias.

At two the next afternoon we stood amongst the huge crowds to watch the floats, carts, coaches and drum and piccolo groups in their artistic costumes. One picture after another presented itself, capturing our eyes and ears, never to be forgotten. The traditional mimosa bunches were thrown to ladies, with oranges and sweeets. From time to time a 'victim' in fun would be hauled up over the side of a waggon by 'Waggis', the loud-voiced, traditional figure from the Alsace, with a giant red wig and nose, wearing wooden clogs, white pants and a blue blouse. Wherever he turns up, he tells people off in the French-German Alsace dialect, causing shrieks of laughter.

I met Tobias again in a tiny old wine restaurant called Liesettli, named after the owner, a well known Basel character who was much loved and respected, and was known to throw out of her bistro customers she didn't approve of. I learned all this, and much more about Basel and its customs and charm, that evening. Tobias and I liked each other instantly. He said I was his *Fasnacht-Schatzeli* and that it was 'Fasnacht fever' and harmless fun.

I had just turned seventeen and had another year's work at commercial school after this first *Fasnacht* experience.

The dreaded diploma was looming. I was apprehensive and told Tobias about it as he walked to the train with me on that last Fasnacht morning.

My train left at six. At times we walked ankle deep in confetti. A hazy mist wrapped Basel in a flattering pale grey, bringing out the pink, turquoise, yellow, green and pale blue of every single little paper circle, like coloured snow. Trams, squeaking and clanking round railed corners, seemed out of place after three days, and clashed painfully with the music of the occasional drum and piccolo players who could not bear to stop. Here and there a tiny group, lost now in the morning traffic, still meandered in twos and threes – Pierrots, clowns and crinolined ladies. Masks loomed in slow motion on unreal figures. A plaintive farewell to Fasnacht and me.

Tobias faced me, as the train pulled in. He had two shining steel milk funnels attached to his chest, like spikey mock breasts, and copper pan-cleaners as flat epaulettes on his shoulders. The rest of him was covered in hundreds of tiny bits of green, gold and silver foil, cleverly cut and stuck so as to make a shimmering, glittering, crackling-sounding armour. This colourful outfit accentuated his dark hair and eyes. He awkwardly crushed me to all this stiff glory, kissed me hotly, then waved me off. Bewildered, I waved enthusiastically till I saw no more of his shine in the awakening morning sun. Gone! A dream!

Somehow I got through the last year of commercial school and passed the exams. After the presentation of the diploma, it was time to say goodbye and leave for Basel. It was also time to face my fears of the office and start earning my own living.

I looked so infuriatingly young that people in shops still called me 'du', instead of the polite form, 'sie', with which adults are addressed. In cinemas, where the age of admittance is sixteen, I was often asked how old I was. I was eighteen and, as ever before, yearning to be able to stay with my mother. I begged to be allowed to live at home. I promised I'd look for work, but secretly I knew I was stalling for time. They agreed. Still not married, they had become used to their life together. They were very much in love and happy. Andreas spoiled my mother. He never came home without flowers, chocolates or different magazines and journals, which they read in bed together while munching chocolates. Rex, in his basket, slept beside them. I used to go and sit on Mother's bed and tell her about my day. These were happy hours. Andreas called Mummy all kinds of special, tender, loving nicknames. They held hands, teased and laughed.

It was a happy household, except when Mummy fell into one of her moods, which were frequent and unexpected, and mostly brought on by me. It was always about a crumb, or dust, or a drop of water in a sink, an unwashed cup in the kitchen or a piece of clothing not tidied away. After a meal, I had to hurry and get the carpet-sweeper and clean around the table. If I remained seated too long, or missed a crumb, it could on certain days unleash a storm of fury, ending with Mother not speaking to me for hours, sometimes for days.

The incident was usually made up the following way. Totally deflated by my mother ignoring me and looking stern, cold and hurt, I'd first pretend I hadn't noticed. Next I'd pretend that it didn't bother me. Then I'd cry all night, till Andreas came to my bedside at three or four in the morning to hug me and tell me to say I was sorry. In the silence after, I could hear him talking to Mother. The next day I'd go and say sorry, and we'd hug and I'd cry some more. If I was lucky, we'd be friends for a week or two, but soon all would be repeated in exactly the same way. I was always the one to apologise, but I hated it because I couldn't understand why my mother made me so miserable, so often, over such idiotic trifles. I loathed her power over me. Thus, as good as it was to be home with my mother, it was also quite frightening and never easy for long.

One evening we were invited to a party. One of Basel's best-loved painters, Charles Hindenlang, was celebrating his sixtieth birthday. (His wife had a small café in Basel, 'The Hollywood' where the three of us often had a snack before or after a movie.) I was only slowly getting to feel at home in Basel. It was in fact completely different from the free-and-easy impression I'd gained during the three days and nights of the carnival. I knew very few people and my old schoolfriends, Yvette and Peter, were away.

As we walked into Charles's studio, I saw Tobias.

We were both surprised and pleased. We talked all evening and he invited me for dinner the week after. He took me to the Walliser Kanne, a chalet-like restaurant.

It was my first real date with a man. Ivo had been my teacher and we'd sort of slipped into going out together. This was my first real invitation and I hoped to be able to forget Ivo for a few hours. I was so nervous and excited that I made Mummy and Andreas laugh by changing my clothes at least ten times before going back to the dress I had first chosen. I wore my long unpermed hair in a smooth, dark blond pageboy, longer at the back. My side parting made my hair shimmer light blond over the top. People thought it was dyed. I hardly wore any makeup, remembering how Ivo had appreciated the natural look, but I wore high heels, because I was small, and my blue dress accentuated my eyes.

He came to pick me up and I watched him stride up the garden-path steps, two at a time, bringing flowers for Mother and me. He was taller than I; his black hair formed a 'V' on his high forehead over his dark eyes. He had a strong, well shaped nose. I liked the many tiny laugh lines that crinkled all the way up to his ears. It had been the first thing about him I'd noticed.

He looked strong. I watched him as he talked to Mother and Andreas with great ease. I was nervous. After a drink, we left.

In the cosy restaurant he placed a small parcel beside my plate. It was my first good perfume – Madame Rochas.

I ordered only a plate of mountain-dried, paper-thin meat. When I was nervous and didn't know someone well, I still could hardly eat, for the old fear would return to sit in the pit of my stomach and in my throat, ever since the children's home. I explained that I was a small eater. We had so much to talk about that we didn't really notice what we ate. Our first topic was Fasnacht and he told me how he presided over an old clique and that these cliques had been craft-guilds in the old days.

His greatest passion, besides Fasnacht, was flying glider-planes, and his third one football. I was fascinated by his talks about flying, but did not tell him that I could never muster the slightest interest in a handful of men running after a ball, while thousands looked on and screamed their heads off. I told him how I'd much rather kick the ball around myself and how I'd shed tears, one Christmas, on being told that there were no female football clubs. We laughed.

The time passed all too quickly and we wandered through the town, up the cathedral hill to the Münster. We sat on the broad wall and looked over the Rhine and the lights of Basel by night. Soon he drove me home.

As I thanked him, facing him and smiling up, he said, 'I'll walk you to the door.' We stopped in the middle of the path and he said, 'You look very, very beautiful in the moonlight. Good night.' – and as he said this he stroked me gently and quickly across the blond part on the top of my head, adding 'I do love that blond shine there.' Then, with a 'I'll phone you tomorrow,' he turned and ran back to the car.

I went to bed in a dream. It had been a wonderful first evening and I hadn't noticed that we really didn't have very much in common. He'd said that he didn't like classical music and thought concerts were for silly people who sat with their eyes closed, looking stupid while listening to the boring stuff. But later he said, if I could play the piano, that was different. He admired that, because he hadn't a clue. He'd love to sit and listen to me. That conjured up all sorts of romantic family scenes in my mind. No, he didn't have time to read or go to many films. Waste of time. He was too busy. For a moment I'd felt the immense difference between him and Ivo, and yearned almost unbearably for the latter. This longing broke through again and again, but I stifled the memories, telling myself that this dark man here had his feet squarely on the ground. That he was as reliable as a rock. Where Ivo was light and blond and airy-fairy, caught up in the spiritual, this man had no nonsense about him. He would probably come to grips with reality much better. He was solid. Why was I thinking such things? Did I love this man? Love? Oh! I came to the conclusion that night that I would never love anyone again. Not like Ivo. I knew that I'd have to settle for less, but I was determined that I'd never ever get so hurt again.

And anything seemed less scary than having to go and work in an office.

Tobias phoned every day. We'd talk for hours, for much of the time not saying anything of importance. I enjoyed it all, yet missed something but didn't know what.

He sent me drawings and presents and we went out to splendid places. He also took me flying, and I managed not to show how terrified I was; in my mind fear of flying was for dumb, hysterical females; my father's words sounded once more. I had to prove to men that women were better. As he flew acrobatics, frightening loops and stunts, I sat it out heroically. He was very pleased. He took me to football matches where I didn't manage quite as well to conceal my true feelings of boredom. I met his friends at parties and was suddenly part of a crowd of important people. At balls and celebrations I realised that Tobias was well respected. He was always at the top: president of his carnival club, best teacher at the aero club, admired at business for being a 'self-made' man, trained in the USA. He was more than ten years older than I, a most promising young man of thirty. He had always worked hard and saved a good sum for his years. He was charming, clever and handsome. I thought I was in love.

He seduced me, the first time, on the back seat of the car. We were engaged by then, and I thought I didn't have the right to say no. He possessed me with my legs spread out grotesquely over the front seat. He seemed so eager, so desperate, that I felt it would have been cruel not to co-operate. There was always this absolute priority of letting a man have his way as if an impending catastrophe, worse than death, hung over me if I didn't. Why wasn't I flattered and pleased to be wanted so passionately, and why did I feel it had nothing to do with love? He wanted to marry me, didn't he? Did he only want sex of me? What was wrong with me?

The next day I crawled round the house, all sparks of joy squashed out of me. He was a heavy man, and I was sore again, and depressed. What was there to look forward to in life, if that was all that marriage was about? It was so unfair. They had this fabulous urge, these intense feelings that made them push and yell and pant. All I felt was resentful, let down, sore and sick, abused against my will and too weak to do anything about it. And this was to go on for the rest of my life? In all the hundreds of novels I'd read, women loved it. They even wanted it and needed it and enjoyed it as much as men. They all claimed to have orgasms galore, from the first time they were entered to the last. Either I was totally abnormal and unfeeling, or frigid, or the writers were men, or the women liars. It was just as hypocritical as the way married couples in films woke up in the morning, looking gorgeous and kissing, instantly, passionately! What about bad breath and brushing teeth? Why was it that in films people never seemed to have to go to the toilet, or suffer from rashes or eczema or piles or constipation or thrush or discharge, or felt sore 'after'? It all made me feel so different, so alone. It was enough to make anybody miserable.

'Olly, what's troubling you? Didn't you have a good evening with Tobias? I hope you haven't quarrelled? He's so nice.' Mummy came up to me.

I remembered our engagement party. Tobias seemed to love the fact that all our friends were doctors and lawyers and artists. He moved with grace amongst them and felt visibly at home here, but had seemed reluctant to invite his father, as if ashamed of him. He was an *arbeiter* (worker), a term that seemed to be almost a swear word in this country. He adored his mother, whom he called 'a real lady'. His father drank and hadn't done 'well enough'. My mother had insisted that his father be invited. I had rather liked him, with his sad, bloodhound eyes. I had been intimidated by his mother, but liked her too.

'Mummy, last night . . . do I have to . . . do I have to let him . . . now . . . ?'

'*Acht Gott!* Did he want to? I mean, now that you're

engaged, I don't see how you can refuse.'

'But Mummy, do I have to, in the back of the car?'

'I – oh dear! I suppose now that you're engaged. . . . Don't you? . . .'

'Mummy, it hurts and I don't feel a thing.'

'Oh, dear! Doesn't he know how and where to use his hands? Many men don't, and believe in the myth of the vaginal orgasm. You'll have to teach him, in time.'

'D'you mean to say that it's not the normal way . . . what you just said?'

'Well, women should be prepared, helped, by foreplay. You can read about it in books. There are no frigid women, only blundering, ignorant men. It always depends on the man, how sexy a woman is. Maybe you can recommend a book to him?'

I wouldn't know how to begin to tackle a subject like this. With Ivo it had been nice, before he'd penetrated me. Then, often, it hadn't been pleasurable, except for that last, sad, unique time.

Soon after this talk, I began to be violently sick in the mornings. Andreas whisked me off to a friend who was a gynaecologist. He confirmed that I was pregnant. Mother and Tobias and Andreas were shocked to a point I couldn't comprehend. They had all been silently in agreement about 'letting us do it', and now they were clamouring about 'the shame'. All I could think of was Ivo saying '. . . Helene has a broader pelvis. . . . It's the motherliness that attracts me. . . . You don't look as if you'd be a mother of six. . . .' and the fear I had since, hoarded deep inside, that I could never have a baby.

Now, all I could do, when I wasn't throwing up, was cry, 'I want my baby! I want my baby! I want my baby!' But Tobias and Mother and Andreas kept going on about 'the shame', 'the degradation', 'the family shame', and how people would point at us and mock and say, 'They had to get married.' Tobias insisted that Andreas should use his friends and organise a solution.

The white-clad, imposing professor convinced me that I was small for my age, underdeveloped, my womb small, making an abortion a must. There was too great a risk. I was taken to hospital after a psychiatrist friend signed the necessary papers. They operated. The nuns seemed to look at me disapprovingly, or did I imagine it? I was really frightened now that I might never be able to have children.

Tobias came to visit. He brought me a green pullover. I hated green. He also brought me an orange lipstick because he disliked my pink ones. I hated his gifts, but I smiled dutifully and thanked him over-enthusiastically to cover my intense disappointment. When he left I relaxed. I had been 'a good girl' once more. I felt in love with Tobias when I could hold his hands and look romantically into his beautiful eyes.

The night before the wedding I prayed, because I was full of fears, 'Please, God, let there be an earthquake.'

But there wasn't.

Chapter Thirteen

I soon realised that if one of the worst surprises in my life had been my father, my new husband was only a little less upsetting. The first three weeks of our marriage were a shock. I was alone every evening till late at night. Sitting. Waiting. Walking up and down. Angry. Hot and frustrated in bed. Isolated, alone and bewildered, unable to turn anywhere because we were expected to be 'newly-wed and happy'.

Every day the effort of cleaning, shopping and cooking a three-course midday meal had me exhausted; coping with household money was beyond me. His mother asked, 'Do English housewives air their beds every morning? Swiss duvets have to be shaken like Frau Holle. You know the fairytale? Pillows thumped. A Swiss *Hausfrau* has her bedding over the windowsills before the husband goes to work. No dust under the beds, nor in corners! You have a lot to learn. You must go to woman's work school, because Tobias needs perfect shirts and razor-edge creases down his trousers to climb the ladder of success.'

'How long do you take over ironing a shirt?' I was asked at the woman's work school. 'Only quarter of an hour? Not good enough! Nothing to be proud of.' I was shown exactly how to iron a shirt, and it took more than twenty minutes. I was told that only after much practice would I do it in less time and perfect enough! I tried hard to master the new skills expected of me.

I phoned his mother and asked for his favourite meals. At 12 o'clock he'd come rushing in, go straight to the dining table and there sit and wait. I'd scurry around, fighting with last-minute obstacles. His silent waiting made me nervous. He'd complain about the soup if it was Maggi, out of a packet — not as good as his mother's. By the time I served the dessert, he would be asking me to hurry with coffee, as he was late because of me. In the kitchen I prayed that the drink would be as he liked it, not too thin, not too strong. Afterwards, the incredible mess to clear away! And it would start all over again for the evening meal, from which he would rush away once more, to meet men-friends, after wiping his mouth on a linen serviette which I always found so hard to iron, full of deep, stiff creases.

Why couldn't he come home smiling? Maybe with flowers or a surprise, chocolates or a book or something to encourage me, as I'd never cooked or done any of this work before? Why couldn't he stand in the kitchen and chatter, admiring how much better I was managing, help carry plates in to save time, joking if things didn't turn out perfectly, instead of scolding, or talk to me about his work, a part of his life about which I knew nothing? Why could he not forget about the boring newspaper which took up every precious second of our togetherness? Why didn't we lie on the couch and kiss and cuddle before he rushed away?

I dreamed of escape, and asked if we could go hitch-hiking together like other young people of my age were doing. He scorned the idea and made fun of my immature fancies. He was old and sensible, compared to me.

It didn't seem long ago that my Father had shot himself, had done horrifying things that I was reminded of at night. I thought marriage would be carefree and full of shared fun, growing closer. Less alone. After another lonely weekend I told myself I had to share his interests, and asked to learn to fly one of the gliders at his club. (He flew every weekend and taught.) I nearly died with fright on my first solo flight. After making myself go up seven more times, I became pregnant and could stop flying without admitting my fears.

He continued going out alone, and I continued to be lonely. Once I aked him to take me out to a meal because it seemed such a long time since I'd sat down to one. He took his newspaper along and hid behind it at the other side of the table. I went to the toilet and then home. That night, when he came home, was the first time we had a big row.

The second time we rowed, he beat me. This was after having been invited to my parents' house with some archaeology friends of theirs. Tobias listened to a football match on the radio, noisily, while we were trying to hold a civilised dinner conversation. I complained about his manners on the way into our apartment. He advanced upon me with fiery eyes and, with the edge of his hand, began to hit me on the side of the head, my jaw, my eyes, my mouth, till I went down on the yellow stone floor.

When I came round, I saw him sitting on the couch in the living room, reading the newspaper. Blood was trickling out of my mouth. I tried to ring my parents but he screwed off the bottom part of the receiver and locked me in the bedroom. I climbed out of the window in such a state that I ran out on to the main road with my eyes closed, hoping a car would instantly end my misery. Nothing happened. I walked to see some friends who advised me to go to a doctor and record what had happened, for a divorce. I didn't, out of fear, also not wanting to admit to failure and out of some sort of loyalty as well. I'll regret all my life that I didn't take their advice.

When I became pregnant, I hoped for a daughter to change our lives. He wanted a son, for flying and for football. I didn't understand why the thought of a boy terrified me. My father had made me feel inferior because I was a girl. Tobias made me have the same negative feelings about myself. If I had had a penis when I was small, Father couldn't have abused me the way he did. If he hadn't had one, he couldn't have disgusted me so much with it. Maybe this is the reason I often dreamed, during my pregnancy, that I saw baby boys whose penises were cut off. I'd wake up sobbing. It seemed that my husband had power over me; he also had 'that thing'. I was terrified of men, boys, penises, but tried so hard to become 'normal'.

I longed for Ivo with a constant, tearing yearning. It was a yearning from the body, mind and heart. To feel once more such a sense of belonging and oneness. When he held my hands, listening to Mozart or Hindemith, I was at peace because he was in the same room. And to be once more so stimulated in the mind! To think, discuss and be alive. Now I felt that I was dead, for time had stood still from the moment I had stepped into this expensively decorated apartment my father's money had paid for. Within these walls I felt as if I had been buried alive, stripped of all fun and youth, from one moment to the other. Except for my baby, growing inside me, life had no meaning. There was no closeness nor tenderness; no sharing.

Birth! I thought I was being ripped apart. I felt the doctor kneeling on my stomach. I yelled and pushed, and the next thing I knew, I had a lovely baby daughter. A beautiful, healthy, wonderful little girl. Nothing could ever go wrong now. Yet, holding her close, I was baffled because I didn't know her. She was a unique and total little stranger. I didn't know one had to get to know one's own babies. I laughed and said, 'Hello, little stranger. I'm delighted to make your acquaintance.' Tobias said, 'You and your funny English sense of humour. Congratulations. You were very brave.'

He brought me blue cornflowers, which I loved, another orange lipstick, and a green plaid skirt to match the green pullover that he had given me for the abortion, and which I had never worn. His father gave me a magnificent gold bracelet and I was deeply touched.

I wondered if from now on I'd be able to enjoy lovemaking with Tobias. Earlier I had come to the conclusion that women were men's 'apple graters'; Tobias regularly grated himself to a moaning climax on me – then fell off, leaving me squashed, messy and alone, while he slept instantly. Sometimes he touched me tenderly but only when he wanted sex. Was this the 'joy of sex' my father had trained me for? Was 'love' hidden in the three dutiful pat-pat-pat's of my husband's nightly staccato hand applications?

In the hospital I learned how to care for the baby, whom we called Arlette. When I got home, I kept running to see if she was still breathing. I was nervous and tense and afraid to do something wrong. After a week, my milk reduced and I was exhausted. For ten days I went home to stay with my mother. She was just as inexperienced and tense, but a friend of hers in the neighbourhood came and helped. She showed us what tough things babies really were. To see her handle Arlette helped enormously and I went home feeling much more self-assured.

It was such a joyful responsibility. I loved every minute with my daughter, but the new demands and the constant pressure and great expectations of Tobias and his family made me unable to cope.

The comparison with their efficiency and perfection kept me in constant nervous frenzy. They had their own washing-machines in their own houses. I had the use of the apartment-house one every two weeks. Coping with nappies was tough and a smelly business. Piles of washing and ironing tugged at my tired nerves. The baby demanded constant attention and I lost many a night's sleep, which caused me to lag in my newly developed skills. My whole home was slipping, not up to Swiss perfectionistic standards, and I was scolded. No one except my Mother helped and she had her own life to lead, after all.

One evening Tobias sat down with me and prepared small envelopes into which he put household money for each day. I tried so hard but sometimes to save time, I'd buy food for three days, borrow money from other days' envelopes and got myself into trouble. I was hopeless. The less I could manage, the less I could face all the chores, and the more I grew tired, listless, apathetic and depressed.

I knew Tobias preferred men's company. It made me slide back down into my deep pit of 'woman worthless' feelings. He didn't show much interest in the baby and I was sure it was because she was 'only a girl'. All we were good for was to serve, to slave and then, after holding still for a bit of self-satisfactory sex, be pushed out of the way. We had no rights to voice our wishes, were uninteresting and a bore to be with. When he gave me his three short smart taps on the head or shoulder, which was his way of saying 'goodnight', I turned over and silently wept. How much worse it was to be alone alongside someone, than totally alone.

I started to get babysitters and go to see films. Mother and Andreas liked to be on their own, so I didn't want to intrude too often. Yvette went out with me, and occasionally we'd spend an evening together, but seeing other couples hand in hand made me feel worse. Coming home to an empty flat was the most depressing thing. At times, I'd wait behind the house till Tobias came in, till the babysitter left, so that he would see what it was like, but he was nasty when I went out alone and it didn't help our marriage.

The many phone calls that came for him made me feel left out and unwanted. He had a brother and a sister and a traditional, conservative Swiss family. He was important in the carnival-'clique', the aero club and at his workplace. He was in demand. After I finished my housework and duties as a mother, my evenings were empty.

Looking in the mirror, I saw that I was young, that I wasn't ugly and yet that my life was over at twenty. Nothing but hopelessness and boredom loomed ahead. I used to sit next to the cot and talk to my little girl, and feel very, very alone. She was no comfort nor company yet, and Tobias didn't share. This didn't feel like a family; I was not part of one. There was no mutual ground, nothing supportive, no hope, no future, no point of understanding, no togetherness, nothing.

Time seemed to stand still and I felt that I'd rather die. Slowly I was becoming indifferent to whether Tobias went out or stayed at home. I got so low that I kept finding myself in front of the bathroom cabinet, pouring all the pills that I had into one hand. Once I remember looking at myself in the mirror and saying, 'Don't. You have no right to! You have a little girl.' But the mirror image said, 'She'd be much better off without you. You're no good to anyone.'

I had run and picked her up. She looked so sweet in her cot, wide-eyed, plump-cheeked, making gurgling noises. Why was there no one to share this joy? I hugged her close and said, 'I'll never leave you, my little one.' I kissed her and said, 'I love you, but I feel so useless. So helpless and alone.' I put her down and saw that there was a hole above her knee in her woollen tights – a hole that hadn't been mended. As I looked, I remembered all the things that I should do, and mend and sew and iron and wash and buy and clean and cook and bake and prepare and catch up with. I went to bed with three sleeping pills, for I knew that if Tobias came home, late as usual, I'd lie there, waiting, fretting, becoming more and more frustrated, angry and envious.

The next morning I overslept and Tobias was bad-tempered. We had another fight. For the rest of the day I took my baby to bed and stayed there, reading trash. Escaping. Forgetting. For 12 o'clock lunch I made soup out of a packet and opened a tin of ravioli. He complained bitterly, as I knew he would. I said I wasn't feeling well. He said he'd expect something better for dinner that night, and left. I always seemed to be crying. I phoned for a babysitter and went to town.

Walking round in a daze, I longed for somebody, anyone to talk to me, touch me, like me and love me.

Someone did!

He was Hungarian. Not specially nice – even dirty – but he smiled at me and I felt like a real person. He talked to me and wanted to get close. I didn't know how to say 'no'. When I'd done it, I felt so bad that I went home and told Tobias. He made me write out a confession and sign it.

'If ever you insist on a divorce, you'll lose the child and I won't have to pay you a penny. You're not only a rotten Swiss housewife and a bad mother, you're also a slut and a whore.' He was beside himself with rage and disgust.

Often I'd put letters on his pillow, telling him how I wanted to love him and what I thought a marriage should be like. I told him how unloved and inferior I felt. Asked him to share an interest with me. To build up some new joined form of sharing, of communicating, doing something, anything, together. He thought letters were damned stupid. He yelled that I was stifling his life. He worked all day for us and I was free, so he wanted the evening and the weekends. 'Forget all your English romantic rubbish. You're married to a Swiss in Switzerland.' I said in that case I wanted to leave because I didn't like the Swiss marriage. His black eyes were frightening; a vein ran from his V down his forehead, swelling. I was paralysed with fear.

'No one is going to leave me. Never!' His voice was too low, too controlled. 'I can do the same as Andreas's wife. I can keep you here forever, as long as I want. You'd never get a divorce, and never, never your child. Now, you learn to do as you should, or I'll make life very unpleasant for you.'

I said, 'I hate you! You're no husband. You're a monster. Why did I have to meet you out of all the men on the earth?'

He did the same thing my father had done. He advanced towards me, holding his arm out. He knew I was ready to fight back, but I couldn't get near him, just wriggled like a fish on the end of a line. And then he hit me. I reeled against the wall on the other side of the room. He said, 'I hit my own father under the table because he was drunk.' He left then. Arlette was asleep. I went and looked at her, and cried.

I moped around for days. It was very hard to try to cook good meals. Every ounce of imagination had left me. One day I felt I had come to the end. I Just stood there and said, 'God, please don't let these four walls be the last four walls in my life.' I held my baby close to me and said, 'Please, get me out of here and let this come to an end. I can't stand to be in these walls or look at them one more day.' All that day I kept remembering the night my father had killed my mouse. I'd bought it for sixpence at the animal market, on my way home from school. The urge to possess something warm and cuddly of my very own had been too strong to resist. I planned to keep it secretly. As I had a tight belt round my waist on my school-uniform dress, I pushed it down my front. It felt cosy and less lonely. At home I scurried up to my room to hide it in a shoebox in my wardrobe. I smuggled food and water up before Father came home.

All went well for two days. I'd reverse my dress to pick off all the little black bits and shake them out of the window. Then one night it had happened. Father had come to my bed and heard the mouse scratching. He got up and opened the wardrobe. When he saw what it was he gave me an awful look while putting on his pyjamas and said, 'I said no pets!' He went downstairs, only to return immediately with a pair of tweezers. With one hand he took me by the scruff of my neck and with the tweezers he caught the mouse by its tail. It screeched terribly. He marched the lot of us down the stairs and pushed me in front of the fireplace where he made me watch as he held my secret pet over the red-hot cinders. He made me watch. There was nothing I dared do. There was never anything I could do. Not even after, when he made me rub him, there, till my shoulder got sore, and then made me take his thing in my mouth. I nearly choked because I kept seeing and hearing my mouse in my mind and it was all so awful and sad and my tears and snot and his stuff were clogging me up.

I rubbed my shoulder and neck. I was always stiff and hurting there. I looked around and realised that I hadn't shopped and hadn't cooked, except for Arlette's food, and I felt as if I'd never have the strength to cook one more meal. I wondered what Tobias would say if there was no meal ready. I turned the radio on. I felt panic. He would beat me up. A voice sang, 'Tea for two and two for tea, a boy for you and a girl for me,' and I sat down and thought, 'who wants a girl? How could a man happily sing, 'a girl for me'? I saw, in my mind's eye, female sexual parts and felt utterly horrible and dirty and sick. How come people could happily sing they wanted a girl? Girls were bad, were smelly, had blood coming out of them and stank, and were used by men, made sore, and were supposed to love it and be sexy and ask for more, every night, but where was love? I was a girl and that's why all the trouble started, but I had wanted a girl to prove to myself that girls were all right. I looked at my baby and saw that every part of her was beautiful and perfect and clean and lovable, and wondered why it wasn't the same with me, and why my parents hadn't found me as adorable and perfect as I found my baby girl.

He would beat me up. I was afraid. The pain inside! Oh,

the pain and confusion and loneliness. I started to pack in a frenzy. Brought up as I had been in such an authoritarian, restricted manner, I believed I had no rights. No right to make my own decisons. Who was I to dare to think? I just had to do as I was told. I switched off the radio. Knocked myself on the corner of the table. It took courage and energy to make my own decision. I remembered how, the night before my wedding, I'd prayed, 'Please God, let there be an earthquake.'

As soon as we were here in our new apartment, I had found out that Tobias had merely exchanged his mother for his wife. He had carried on his own bachelor life. There was no change for him. For me everything had changed.

I wanted to make a decision. What would Mother say? What would his parents and sister and brother say? And their partners? What would Tobias do? What was I to do? What would happen? The first time I had ever taken a decision of my very own, the result had been the suicide of my father.

Into two suitcases I pushed nappies and baby things. Into my handbag I put my toothbrush. It was about six. In one hour he would be home. I ordered a taxi. As Tobias always drove the Isabella-Borgward Mother had said I should buy with Father's inheritance, I never had the use of a car. I brought Arlette to Mother's house, told her everything and took a taxi to the Friedmatt. This is a lunatic asylum. They are called 'psychology clinics' nowadays, and this sounds less discriminating, though just as frightening. But anything was less scary than me standing in that bathroom with pills in my hands, not wanting to live, when I had such a lovely baby.

As I walked past the flower beds in front of the asylum I remembered myself sitting in a sand-pit in England, and the despair I had felt then. I thought that 'something' inside me was torn and broken at last, much later, only now, at twenty-three! Funny! I didn't die as I thought I would when I was little and played in the sand and missed Mummy.

When I arrived at Friedmatt about eight, I was taken to a huge room. As I had no papers signed by a doctor, I was treated with suspicion. They made me feel like a criminal as they informed me that I had to be bathed, scrubbed and have my hair washed. After the whole humiliating business, which didn't help my wretched condition, I was put into a general ward. Timidly, I managed to say that my period was just starting. I was given an old-fashioned, hand-knitted sanitary towel and a belt of the sort washed every month and reused. Things really seemed behind the moon here, but I wasn't in much of a mood to care.

In the ward were ten beds on each side, occupied by women of all ages: long-haired, short-haired, red, black and blond-haired, some staring, others sleeping. There were bars at the windows. They locked the door behind me. As I crawled under the bedclothes, wondering what I'd let myself in for, my cramps began. . . .

A voice woke me. 'What on earth are you doing here?' It was a professor who knew Andreas and Mother. He immediately ordered a different room for me and I had a good breakfast before I had to go to him.

My talks must have been confusing, for I didn't understand what it was that was troubling me. Tobias had told me again and again that we had a good apartment, a car, a child, clothes, food, everything.

'You must be mad not to appreciate what we have, or plain ungrateful. What more do you want?' I didn't know.

'Just to be together more,' I had answered vaguely. He'd shouted, 'You wouldn't be satisfied if I pulled my hair out for you!'

Now, seeing it all from a distance, I didn't know what I had run away from. I mean, he'd only really hit me twice and probably I had provoked him and deserved it. I had a good life, really? My sister-in-law could cope so well and had two small children. Why couldn't I? What on earth was the matter with me? I began to cry and couldn't say anything that made sense. I only saw how I'd lost Ivo, and how I'd ruined everything with Tobias. I was a slut and a whore and now here I was in a lunatic asylum instead of with my child. I'd never make it. Was a failure, as Father had always said. Over and over again, I failed in everything I did. It just happened. I never noticed how I got myself into these messes. It just happened.

The doctor used a lot of medical and technical terms I couldn't understand. Not wanting to appear stupid, I nodded all the time. He then gave an order for me to be given insulin treatment. It consisted of pills and a terribly sweet drink in the mornings. So I sat around in my room, sat around elsewhere in the asylum. I went for my meals, then sat in the lounge, all the time wondering what I was doing here.

In the garden there was a black raven in a cage.

They brought an old woman to sleep in my room. In the night she started to scream. Kneeling in the middle of the room, tearing her pyjamas off, she scratched at her withered long breasts, chanting, 'Oh dearest Mother Mary, have mercy!' She kicked and yelled as they pulled her out of my room.

The next night they brought a young girl. She climbed into my bed as I slept, to cuddle up beside me. She woke me, told me she needed warmth and skin-contact because she was a lesbian. I explained, politely so as not to hurt her feelings, that I wasn't a lesbian and preferred to have a bed to myself.

The night after, something started itching in my pubic hair. It nearly drove me insane. I went to a toilet to examine myself and found little black spots. I pulled one out in horror and placed it carefully on to a sheet of white toilet paper. The thing moved! It had legs! I had picked up 'felt lice' from the hand-knitted sanitary towel that had not been clean. This I was told later by the gynaecologist I asked to go and see. He said the eggs must have been in there. I nearly died with the disgust and shame. He gave me a white ointment and I was soon clean and back to normal and rid of the nasty things.

Mother and Andreas came to tell me that Tobias had arrived at their place, barged in and ripped Arlette out of my mother's arms and taken her away. He said she would be brought up at his sister's, and that is where he wanted her to stay. I went into shock when they told me this. I had never thought how things might turn out. I had acted in a state of semi-consciousness.

They told me they would get me a good lawyer. And soon I had to go and see him. Naively I said, 'I have nothing terrible to say about my husband. I want a divorce. We're like oil and water. It doesn't mix. He is a nice person, I'm a nice person, so let's settle it all decently in friendship. We made a mistake, so let's solve it.'

The lawyer informed me that this way I could never get divorced. Only would it be possible if I brought out all the dirty washing into the open.

It was the most tormenting, lengthy procedure. He was curt, cold and to the point. There was no room for any feeling, no glimpse of humanity. He'd pound question after question at me and get irritated with my replies. They were never precise and short enough. I detested going up the dark stone stairs to his dingy old office.

I stayed at Friedmatt for three months. Christmas and New Year nearly broke my heart, it was so lonely there. My little girl was now one-and-a-half, and I'd missed her first steps. On Christmas Day, Louise, Tobias's sister, brought her to see me. My Arlette reached out with both arms the minute she set eyes on me. I rushed over and hugged her to me. We clung and cried. She pressed her little face into the side of my neck. She wouldn't let go for a second. We huddled together on a chair in the austere visitors' room. When our time was up, and Louise tried to put on her tiny red duffle-coat, Arlette screamed and made herself stiff till she went blue in the face. They had to tear her away from me.

That evening, around the Christmas tree, I watched the pathetic simpletons, the spastic, the moaning, screeching, twisting lot; later, in my ward, the depressed, the silent and the apathetic. I wondered what had gone wrong with God's creation and wondered if this would be different if they hadn't nailed Him to the Cross. Christmas! Under the tree, decorated only with undangerous, harmless, unshiny bits and pieces, the nurses and helpers were dancing on New Year's Eve. I watched some women kiss and hug and fumble together. I missed my little girl.

I had no aims, no sense of direction or motivation. What was the sense of being here? What was the sense of ever getting out?

Chapter Fourteen

I had been in the asylum about two months when Mother, on one of her visits, told me that a friend of hers was in a play on one of the Basel-dialect comedy stages. The group needed a young girl for a part. As I could look about fourteen when I chose to, they wondered whether I would like to play the small part. The idea made me nervous, but acting was something I'd always wanted to do, so during my last month at the asylum, I got a pass to go to rehearsals.

I still had that 'left out' feeling when I had to be with people, and I was sure they always saw what a freak I was. On top of all the mess, I was now someone from the 'loony bin'. However, I did exactly as I was told and on my first, opening, night, everything went very well. I had to push a bicycle from the right over the stage to the left, and say 'Good evening, Father.' In the second scene I had to push the bike from left to right and say 'Goodbye, Father'. I thought it was the greatest part anyone had ever played, and everyone told me that I walked very naturally!

Mother came to say that I could return to live with her and Andreas in a month. She also told me that Louise had cleaned out my apartment, taking home all the dirty washing and ironing to do in addition to her own. (God, how inadequate these wonderful Swiss women always made me feel!) Louise was now caring for my child as well as her own two small ones. Mother had heard that the furniture in our apartment would be split up later. I felt no regrets. Looking back, there seemed nothing worthwhile to remember about my brief marriage. The only ache and worry was about Arlette, but my lawyer was going to take care of everything, I had been assured. That's what he was paid for, and if Andreas had insisted on him, he must be a good man, I believed.

During the last year of my marrige I had occasionally wondered what sort of work I would have liked to do, if I had been able to freely choose for myself. I had decided that the thing I liked doing best was moving to music. I had always been best at gym. About this time I saw an advertisement by a Basel school of gymnastics and noted the phone number. After my success on stage (for in the newspaper reviews, the critics had called me 'a refreshingly natural young girl'), I had gained a fraction of self-confidence. I was informed that the training to become a gymnastics teacher would take three years; the diploma thus attained would enable me to teach privately or at schools, or for continuing-education classes.

I went for an interview, and was accepted. From then on I seemed to run and run, as if to forget how much I missed my daughter. For the time being I was permitted to see Arlette once a month, because it was held that more frequent meetings would upset her too much and she would not be able to settle. It was a heartbreaking situation for us both. When the crying and tearing away was over, I used to escape into non-stop action.

I started my training at the Basel Conservatory for Music, where the gymnastics training also took place. I spent four to five hours a day there. Besides that, I was asked to take on a part in Basel's Fauteuil Theatre, and I eagerly accepted. I wanted Tobias to give me the car, which my money had purchased, because I now lived far out of town with Mother, but he opposed this, saying that he had paid for the car's upkeep during the last two years. I had just enough money left from my father's estate to pay for the gym training, some clothes and a small, secondhand Topolino car. I worked out that if I budgeted carefully, I would be able to see myself through. I didn't have to pay board for the first year I stayed at Mother's. I often bought flowers, meat or chocolates, or invited her and Andreas out for a meal.

The opening night at the Fauteuil was terrific. I really lived the part. I played Monica, a young, unhappy girl. The critics were enthusiastic and I was ecstatic. 'Olivia played her part superbly and with great sensitivity. She was especially good during the long, silent times, where she was present and contributing in a specially touching way. For a first part, it showed great promise . . .'

I couldn't quite believe it, and danced with joy round Mother after I had taken the review to show her.

'That'll show those snobs who are always trying to tread us down,' she said. (When Tobias had snatched Arlette from her after I left for the asylum, he had said, 'My child cannot stay under a roof where people live together in sin.')

After that play, I was asked to take the main part in another play called *The Quarry*, that was touring Switzerland and Germany for three months. The salary was high, and hotel and travel expenses were paid. As most of the tour fell into the holiday break at the music academy, I accepted.

On this tour I met some interesting people like Leopold Biberti and Maria Schell and Alfred Rasser, and learned a great deal. I also suffered often because I didn't know how to defend myself against all the smooth people of the acting profession. My friend Yvette brought Arlette to me on our weekends, or I drove for hours before and after the performances to be with her. It was a great honour to play on such stages as the Zürich-Schauspiel-Haus. I received consistently good reviews. In one village I even met a lady who came backstage and claimed to have been one of my first nannies, in Basel. In Zürich I saw the woman who had been my nanny in the Bradford days (Gross-mamma's daughter) and who had noticed my name advertised and came to see the play. Afterwards she came to the dressing-room and fell upon my neck. She had three girls of her own now. Switzerland seemed full of old nannies of mine!

Later the whole play was televised and I appeared on two magazine front-pages, in colour. I was photographed high on a ladder, with balloons, and the caption read, 'Switzerland's new and promising young actress, Olivia. With luck and charm she started the year. Let's hope it continues that way.' But it didn't. For, just as strangely and miraculously as the much-desired acting career had suddenly got under way, so it came to a standstill. No one asked me to audition. No one had money or plays or the possibility of plays. I concluded that my acting career had been 'just one of those things'.

At this time all I really wanted was to have my little girl with me. My darling Arlette, who, every time I had to leave her, every time she even saw her coat being readied, fell on the floor, stiff and screaming till she went blue and almost seemed to stop breathing. I would gladly have given up everything to have been able to have her with me, and to start my life all over again, with her. How I loved and missed her! I consoled myself with plans for our future together, once the divorce was granted. I was quite convinced that when this happened, I would be able to start a new life with my daughter.

Louise and her husband were cool and condescending when I went to pick up Arlette from them every third weekend. I would go to the zoo, or do something special with her, and then go back home to Mother's house. Andreas and Mother adored her and she loved being with them. I had never realised how quickly babies grew into proper little people, nor that there was a life outside my marriage and that time does not stand still. Looking back, I sometimes wondered why I had become so stuck, and if it could have grown into something wonderful if I had stayed. What had I done?

I got a letter from Val Arnolds. She still had my watch. She said she missed me and loved her life in England. Her letter sounded as if it came from a different planet. The English certainly knew how to enjoy life. She wrote of parties and boyfriends and fun and sport. She still had a horse and rode. I remembered Yorkshire and wondered what would have happened to me there. If only I had been able to stay. Here everything was so serious; no evergreen songs in the air, no party games, no compliments or teasing, praise or rewards. Even in the English language there seemed to be more encouraging phrases than in that of our country: 'Jolly good!' 'Keep it up!' 'Good show!' 'Well done!' 'Sorry about that . . .' and 'You do look lovely!' – a generally more polite and caring attitude. Here the word 'fun' was suspect. I still felt like a fish out of water a lot of the time I was here in Switzerland – but I knew I would never be able to go back, because of Arlette.

Val wrote to say that one of her favourite friends, Ashley Brown, was coming to work for the same chemical firm my father had worked for. He would arrive in Basel in a week. Would I show him round, if he phoned me? I found myself looking forward to meeting an Englishman and to speaking English again.

Ashley phoned. He sounded most pleasant, and we agreed to meet in front of the police station in the Aeschen Platz. It was spring and I'd bought a new dress with a white bow trim. I now had a short, wavy hairstyle and was looking better. The gymnatics course had done me a world of good; I was improving all the time and working my muscles hard. In the plaza I could see him from a long way off. He had his back slightly turned and looked very tall. I liked the classical shape of the back of his head. He turned to face me, we both beamed at each other – and simply loved what we saw. It seemed that, from then on, we never stopped smiling. We drove out to the country, to Mother's place. She had prepared a wonderful meal, with candles on the table. We laughed till almost in tears at many English jokes during that dinner.

Everything was perfect – and it stayed that way for a whole year. Ashley adored Arlette. We did fun things together; swam and camped and walked and lay in fields, saw shows and kiddies' films. We were deeply and happily in love. He went back to England for a week and returned to Basel a week before my divorce and my diploma were due to be granted.

One year of legal separation! The strain had been tremendous. The divorce and the diploma almost came together. I passed: anatomy, rhythmics, a routine dance to a piece of music, a class performance and a ball-rope-and-hoop sequence. I passed!

But I was shattered in one blow by the divorce. My lawyer said I was not going to be allowed to speak; he would do the defending. He would fight for me – but as Mother and Andreas lived together without being married, they didn't want to cause too much dust. That time in the old divorce court was a most heartbreaking experience. I had to listen to dreadful accusations and could refute nothing. I was a slut. I didn't put the tops on toothpaste! And I even used a facecloth to wash up with when I had run out of clean dishcloths! I wasn't an efficient Swiss housewife, nor an organised mother. Immature. Bad, bad, bad. I had committed adultery. I was bad. Not fit to bring up a child. That was the result of people who lived in sin together. And as that household would be the only place to which I could take Arlette, and Tobias was not willing to pay me anything so I could set up any other, Arlette would be put into the family of his sister, Louise, unless there was 'a change of situation'. I'll never forget the triumphant look Tobias threw me as he marched past after this verdict.

I met Mother, Andreas and Ashley in a restaurant. Mother said, 'Never mind. We told the lawyer that we couldn't have had Arlette anyway, because we're too old to have a small child around. So don't worry. It's all for the best. You'll be free to teach and carry on with your life, and Arlette will be well looked after, living with two children, and you'll see her every three weeks.'

Ashley said, more sternly than I had ever heard him, 'Don't speak to her like that now. Can't you imagine what it must feel like when you've just lost your child?' I loved him for it. After the meal which I couldn't eat, we both went for a long walk. I cried his shoulder wet. He was kind, gentle and understanding. He just held me close and comforted me, talking softly, wiping my face with his clean hanky.

I was surprised that life went on.

I only lived for those weekends with Arlette. She grew up so quickly, but the separation never became easier. I'd rush to pick her up at twelve on a Saturday, dreading the cool encounter with Louise. I'd hurry away to have her to myself, and we'd hug and kiss and chatter away for all we were worth. We enjoyed every second intensely and used to cuddle in bed in the evening to tell endless stories. Yet each Sunday found us unable to look each other in the eye, because we were so afraid we would start to cry. The Sundays were hard.

My darling little girl. I had so longed to give her a carefree childhood, a happier one than I'd had, but now I had made it even more unbearable. What Tobias had done, by separating us, except for this one weekend a month, was inhumanly cruel. He was punishing me by being cruel to this innocent child. I hated him!

I lived for the holidays Arlette and I spent together. The school holidays were the one stretch of closeness and uninterrupted happiness we both had to look forward to. After my diploma was granted, I took Arlette to Lugano, with Ashley. We had a wonderful time. By the time the next holidays arrived, I had already been earning for some time and wanted to do some travelling. Ashley was back in England. Arlette and I flew to Majorca. She scratched her leg on the plane seat's armrest and said, 'I've scratched all the orange-peel off my leg.' It was a 'family' joke for years to come. The stewardess loved her. The plane flight and Majorca were a big adventure. We had a room overlooking the beach and the garden, wherein grew the first bougainvilleas we had ever seen. Arlette was fascinated by the little purple 'lanterns'. We found a stray kitten, half starved, and smuggled food from the kitchen and secretly fed it. The tears when we had to leave it behind! We met Pierre, who wanted to marry me instantly and adopt Arlette. He was from Paris, but worked in the Sahara Desert. I said I'd never ever get married again. I thought it was the worst invention. If I wanted to bury myself alive, there were easier ways of doing it. There was no offence, and he became a good friend. He drove us in his car, took us to caves, and on boat trips.

In winter I took Arlette on skiing holidays. We went to Mürren, Kandersteg, Lenk, Zermatt and Gstaad. After Majorca, we had summer holidays together in Ascona, Italy, France, Austria and Lake Como. We took a tent or booked on hotel package-deals. We always had marvellous times together.

I'd rather not think about the goodbyes. My life had seemed always to be full of partings; they just went on and on, only now they were the other way round. Previously I had been constantly tearing myself away from my mother. Now I had to do the same to my daughter. Why did this have to happen to me? To her? To us? I yearned and dreamed of being able to speak on a normal basis with Tobias. We weren't the first couple to be divorced. But at the divorce court that day he had proclaimed that from the minute I had walked out, I was dead to him. He had sworn that he'd never speak to me or see me again and he kept his promise.

Now all my jobs and after-work activities were planned around my weekends with Arlette. I only ever missed one. On that occasion I was sick with the flu, and later she related her intense disappointment to me. How she'd waited, as always, and jiggled with impatience, and how all the sunlight had gone out of the sky when she was told Mummy wasn't going to come and get her.

Once, just before Christmas, on one of our weekends with Mother, Arlette developed a temperature and Andreas said she should stay in bed. I phoned Louise, who sounded suspicious. She would have to consult with Tobias, she told me. She phoned back to say that he had ordered the child to be brought home according to her set time with me, otherwise he would come to get her with the police.

We learned to be brave and stifle pain. My only strength and comfort during this time was Ashley. He had signed on in Basel for three more months. We were together again, whenever we could be. Every third weekend we did something especially enjoyable, with Arlette. She adored Ashley. Things could have been right forever, but he asked me to marry him — and I ran. I just ran away and left him sitting in a room.

I went home, locked myself into my room, and didn't know what to do.

He phoned and my mother knocked at my door saying, 'You can't do that to him. He's done nothing but been generous and good. What's wrong with you now?'

'I don't know.'

'He wants to marry you.'

'I know.'

'You've always been clamouring about how you miss England and the English, and now everything is served to you, like a present from heaven, you go mad. Olly, do you know what you want?'

'No! I'm scared.'

'What of! I mean, here is a man in a million. He's offering to fly with you to Yorkshire, has taken you to London, to shows, to the best restaurants in town. You're known at the airports for flying into each other's arms! Everybody's in love with you as a couple. You couldn't do better. He spoils you, has a great sense of humour, adores Arlette, is kind and loving and so good looking. What on earth more do you want?'

'I don't know. I just never want to get married again. Marriage is so awful. It's the worst thing that could happen to anybody. The minute you get married, everything turns into a nightmare. I know.'

'Olly, look at me and Andreas.'

'I saw you and Father.'

'But look at us now,' she almost shouted through the door.

'That's different. It's because you can't get married. I'd live with Ashley forever, but I'll never sell myself to a man and the law again. One minute I'm free. The next the law tells me what to do and what not to do, and whether my child is my own or whether I lose it. No! I'm never, never, ever getting married again, and if he can't love me without that signature, he'll have to go.'

'Olivia! You don't know what you're saying. Don't risk losing or hurting him. He's unique. I've never met such a wonderful person. You'll never get such a chance again. And English! I mean, I can't understand you.'

'I've never understood myself, so give up trying. I'm just no good. A rotten apple. You might as well give me up as a bad job.' I opened the door, 'Oh, Mummy, I'm so miserable! I love him so. I don't want to hurt him.'

She went to the phone and dialled his number and held out the receiver to me.

'Olly?'

'Ashley!' I sobbed. All he said was, 'I'm coming over. I love you.'

He came and we talked for hours, me crying, swollen-eyed. He couldn't understand why his love wasn't enough for me, why it could not make me go, calmly and trustingly, to the ends of the earth with him. I wanted to, so badly, but my fear was greater, although entirely without reason.

He showed me two little wedding rings he had commissioned a goldsmith to make. They were tiny wreaths of ivy. I had never before seen such meaningful symbols of love. I yearned to put them on, but knew I never could. And as this fear was greater than my will, and greater than my love, I hated myself.

A month later he went back to England. I missed him all the time. We went on writing for three yers. Occasionally he sent me tickets to go to London. At these times I felt I had to go. I had to see him. When I arrived I used to race into his arms and he would swing me round, hugging. We smiled, we talked, we loved. We dined and we went to shows; we saw *My Fair Lady*, *Salad Days* and *The Boy Friend*. We ate at Vera Swamis – my first Indian food. We met the High Commissioner for Ghana and his wife at a jazz club. Later this couple took us to their hotel suite, where a magnum of champagne was served us. These visits were all like fairytales. He never mentioned marriage again, but when we looked into each other's eyes, I felt like a traitor.

The relationship continued like this for three years. It was bliss and it was hell. In the meantime, in Basel, I was teaching gym and acting small parts in various theatre groups. I went out with other men I met and tried to prove to myself that I was like them. That I could have sex without love, could beat men at their own game, could have whom and what I wanted and could stay free and independent. All the time I knew that I was cheating Ashley, that I was cheating myself.

Another time I visited England to see him, I spent my first two weeks in Yorkshire again, in his new flat. We went to see all my old favourite childhood places. We stood and looked at Father's house, my sad old home. I got a migraine. Miss Abbott's house was empty. The people next door said she'd died. She had never answered any of my anxious letters. The next day I flew back to be with Arlette, during her weekend, and I knew I couldn't go on in this way. I loved Ashley so much, yet I was hurting this person I loved most in the world, besides my child. Arlette kept asking about him and missing him. I wrote and said that I could never get married to him, because Tobias had custody of Arlette and I could not leave her and go to England. He wrote that we had talked about that a hundred times; that he could work in Basel, or fight and try to get custody of her, once we were legally settled.

Again I went to England. This time I met his parents, who were divorced. We all got on well, sat in front of fireplaces drinking tea and eating muffins and scones. We went to the finest pubs and restaurants on my beloved Ilkley Moors, and I saw how much a part of me all this way of English living was. But I couldn't stay. We slept in a huge double bed and couldn't get close enough. Our love was perfect; it seemed we could do nothing wrong together. Yet as I left, I knew that I could never see him again. His parents were hoping we'd get married, mine were asking all the time, and the question was always in his eyes. It was the saddest parting at the airport, that time. I thought my heart would break, and I knew that he knew.

That last evening, he had taken me to my first prom concert, conducted by Sir Malcolm Sargent, who sang *Land of Hope and Glory* with the audience and the orchestra at the end. I realised then that I loved England with an inexplicable devotion, that it had tradition and unity like no other country I knew, yet I could never belong there.

On my return, I hated to change to the Basel dialect. It sounded strange; I felt the language didn't belong to me. I resented the snappy rudeness of people pushing, not queuing. I hated the bustle and hurry, compared to the stoic calm and manners of England. I hated, hated, hated this Swiss-ness that was also in me. And I knew I was being unfair.

I didn't answer Ashley's letters. I took a new flat, and told Mother to tell him that it was over if he contacted her. One day she brought me a telegram. All it said was, 'Our engagement party is booked at the Averard Hotel. My family and yours are invited. This is my final effort. Come to me, darling.' The date was three weeks away. I telegraphed, 'I love you but can't ever get married. It is over.'

The next two days he drove non-stop through France, and

I knew he was coming. I seemed to sense him getting nearer, mile by mile. I got into my old Topolino, didn't tell anybody of my destination but fled to Mainz where I had friends. They were from a political cabaret group called Arche Noah, Mainz. Their scriptwriter, Hans Dieter Hüsch, was a genius. He was lyrical, poetic and humorous. I'd first seen the group in the small Theatre Fauteuil and went every night after the opening of their *Children from Nagasaki*. The whole group had created storms of enthusiasm in Basel. In the parts that were funny, one could immediately identify with the actors and their comic situations. The mirrors reflecting the mess of our world which they held up to the audience could have made one howl in despair. The way Hüsch accompanied himself on the spinet, the mimicry he had perfected, the subtlety of his scripts, were all incredibly moving. I soon knew their programme off by heart and the players must have seen me sitting in the front row, night after night. We met one evening after the performance, became friends, and I was invited to Mainz by one of the couples.

In the group's presence at Mainz I thought I had found what I'd been looking for: thought-provoking, stimulating discussion; being catapulted into sparkling awareness through the company of thinking, articulate, artistic people. I sat in smoky rooms, didn't get enough sleep, one minute felt lifted high by a burst of insight, the next deflated by a better counter-argument. Once more it was brought home to me that I knew nothing. The longer I stayed, the more my stock of answers dwindled: evolution stood on thin legs, God could not be proven, some of the most intelligent of men went gaga in the end, great thinkers went mad, rich men became bankrupt, or descended from wealth to self-destruction. The life and world that I thought palpitated somewhere out there, and had only to be reached for, to be grabbed and jumped into, didn't really exist.

Reality was brick-hard and bruising, dashed my flimsy dreams to smithereens. There was nothing except satisfaction in the simple little things of life, and even these didn't show themselves for what they were unless I recognised their simple truth. However, I wasn't ready to accept that. I wanted the big world out there, wanted to leave my mark, to prove something – although I hadn't a clue what.

During these Faustian nights in Mainz, Ashley was desperate

back in Basel. Mother later told me she hardly knew how to cope with him. She said he cried like a child and wouldn't accept that he had to give me up. I didn't want to know of his suffering.

After ten days in Mainz, I drove back, a little bit more disillusioned, more alone.

Mother pointed out how coldly and inhumanly I had behaved. She said it had been absolutely terrible for Ashley, as if I'd cut out his heart with a knife, after all he had done and hoped for, all these last three years. I said I couldn't help it. It was over, although I missed him, and always would.

Arlette missed him too. She was now a beautiful little girl, with two pigtails, dimples, front teeth missing and plump red cheeks. Her eyes were green and sparkling. We could laugh and play, but the Sundays were always tearful, and the pain of those evening departures never lessened. We both ended them in heaps of misery. I'd stand outside the closed door of her house and hear her crying and Louise's voice, snappy with jealousy, saying 'I have all the nasty times, the work and the tears. She has a Sunday child, the fun and the games. Eat! Eat up so I can finish my work. We're not only here to serve you. Eat so you can go to bed.'

Oh, how that hurt! Her tone of voice. My little girl.

Chapter Fifteen

I got my work organised. From seven in the morning until noon I taught classes of sport and gymnastics at various schools. These were an ordeal as most of my teenage pupils were taller than I and I had to work hard to tire them out and keep discipline.

On some afternoons I went to old people's homes to do 'keep-fit' work with them, to music, while sitting on chairs. We'd rotate our wrists and ankles and knees, stretch and bend, roll and throw balls to each other, and stand in a circle massaging each other's backs and necks. They loved it, and were a happy lot. In the evenings I'd go to continuing-education schools to teach rhythmic gymnastic courses. On Saturday mornings I had private classes in a studio I rented. At one period I was teaching fifty-two hours of gym a week.

Every time the holiday season arrived, I travelled with Arlette. Only the best was good enough. The rest of the year I was too busy and too tired to think much. I bought many clothes and went to expensive hairdressers. I seemed to need beautiful things, to spoil myself. But all the while I still felt empty.

Fasnacht festivals were my own now, and I'd go to balls with friends, play in *gugge-musiks* and win prizes for original costumes. I'd dance and flirt and shout the loudest, but I couldn't kill what I knew deep inside. I didn't want to know that I wasn't happy. What was happiness anyway? And from where did I get the ridiculous notion that we were entitled to such a thing? Life was a mess; a stretch of fate, full of better or worse coincidences, to be endured any way one could.

I went on like this, kidding myself that I was free and therefore fine, for another ten years. I had ups and downs, inner battles where I managed to strangle my conscience more and more. I looked back at my childhood, back at the heaps of 'broken glass' in my life, and blamed my mother. Why hadn't she noticed what my father had done? Why had she always sent me away? Why hadn't I had a family, caring, loving, like everyone I knew? Why did I still always feel the odd one out? Why?

I resented my mother, resented having to be a 'good girl' for her, resented having to say and feel what I knew she expected, to do or not to do what she wanted or didn't want me to do while I was in her house, or when I was with her. She still used to give me that horrified, strict, 'Don't Olivia!' look, and could make me squirm in an instant. I felt she was still in control and had total power over me. Me free? What was freedom? My life seemed too limited, my mind was trapped. Often I felt like bashing my head against a wall. Where was I going and what for?

Sometimes art could absorb me completely. In a good film like *Beauty and the Beast* by Cocteau, or *Les Enfants du Paradis*, I'd feel something igniting inside, pressing to get out. I would see the violence and threat of war in this world. I hated all lack of sensitivity, hated what Tobias and I had done to each other and to our child. I thought about what men had done to each other in wars, and had done to helpless animals. Why could there not be only love and beauty, humour and good feelings? Why jealousy and possessiveness, impossible expectations and rivalry? I would sit through Mozart's *Magic Flute* and cry with sheer admiration that one man could have created such splendour and purity. To me, more than any other composer, Mozart had 'conquered suffering'.

After such experiences I'd usually come down with a bang. I'd either find an unpaid bill waiting for me at home, or have trouble with a schoolgirl class not behaving. Or I'd try to wash some of Arlette's clothes specially well, because I was still under criticism and condemnation because of my lack of domestic abilities, and something would discolour or shrink. Ironing her things made me tense. The voice of the judge would be in my ear 'She leaves the top off the toothpaste. Takes a facecloth for a dishcloth.' Or I'd hear my in-laws 'Don't women in England air the beds or make them with perfect corners?' These memories could still torment me. I despised myself for never being able to pick up a dishcloth or a toothpaste tube now without remembering and hurting.

We had a new director at one of the evening schools and I had to go and meet him. At the same time I'd met a wonderful woman who attended one of my classes. She was a Pisces, like myself, and we really liked each other. Her name was Claire. She was older than I, with a long auburn ponytail. She moved gracefully and we started practising folk-dances together. On my free weekends we choreographed and danced for many happy hours. This was my first really creative experience. We used to perform at family gatherings and weddings, or at evening functions, and we got much praise and applause. It was a new outlet and joy, and I began to earn well.

I made friends with many of my other clients and pupils and began to slowly feel at home in Basel. As my schedule became too strenuous for my body, and I developed backache, I changed some evenings and mornings for English language classes. I arranged this with the new director. He was looking for English teachers and I said that I spoke it more fluently than the Basel dialect. The English classes were great fun and I taught them for more than ten years. Many friendships also developed in them. I was beginning to collect people like stamps.

The new director of the evening school, whose name was Roland, asked me out to dinner. I remember going to sleep at Claire's place afterwards and ranting and raving about him. He was tall, thin and dark, with intense blue eyes. Claire and I had a dancing performance a few days later, and he came to watch. We started going out together and he asked me to accompany him to Greece the next Easter. As it was Tobias's turn to have Arlette that Easter, I agreed; I had never been to Greece.

The country's beauty overpowered me. Athens! A sunny city with the Acropolis shining on the heights above. The warmth and friendliness of people in the old part of the town here, and on the many islands we later visited, added to the joys of each new day. Mikonos was a gem of an island to sail up to: windmills and whitewashed houses against a brilliant blue sky; a pet pelican waiting on the shore to greet every tourist. At Ios, a tiny island with one windmill and one hill, donkeys were used for transport up and down the narrow streets. Here people came out of their white houses to greet us and offer accommodation and food, and the smiles of the beautiful children won our hearts.

Olympia! I'll remember always the flowers blooming among the ancient white pillars and figures, the serene cyprus trees, the almost reverent peace of the place, and over all the incredibly bright light which is said to be different from anywhere else in the world. Roland and I sat in front of the tiny museum there and witnessed the amazing struggle of some huge brown ants as they worked in the coarse yellow sand. A special joy was the sea, so unique for us inhabitants of the mountainous, land-locked, mini-country that is Switzerland.

And in the midst of this Greek holiday, from one second to the next, my companion went insane!

We were on the island of Kos. There, in front of my startled eyes, Roland turned from a blue-eyed happy, smiling man into a black and frowning satan, hair literally standing on bristly end at the back of his neck. He dashed on to a rock the camera Andreas had lent him, then tore into our cottage room and there smashed everything that he was able to lay hands on. I was taken by utter surprise and was frightened. Who was this man?

I fled to a small fishermen's restaurant in the village, and tried to collect my thoughts. What had happened? We had been sitting on the beach talking about Claire, after spending the morning walking and then reading aloud to each other. As I was telling him Claire's sad love story, from which she had never recovered, he had suddenly shouted, 'To hell with Claire and the boring tale of her old lover. I've been divorced three times and have three illegitimate children as well as five from my marriages. To hell with your petty stories! You don't even know who you're with. I've such heaps of failures behind me, you would scream. And who do you think you are, dancing these national dances with rows and rows of Greeks, smiling at all of them, always in the circle while I'm out!' Then he had begun to cry and it was awful to hear the gulps and wrenching sobs as he smashed the camera on to the rock. As he ran from me he had said, 'I'm always on the outside, looking in on life through glass walls.'

Upset and uncertain, I was ready to leave, but compassion brought me back. That night I comforted him, rocking him on my lap, huge as he was, and crooning to him as to a child.

He told me how this happened again and again. He was always looking in on life. He needed different partners, but had to destroy them when he couldn't copy them. If his partner acted, he wanted to be an actor, if she wrote, he wanted to be a writer, and if she danced, he wanted to dance. But he was too old, and not creative, so he could never achieve his desire and then he began to hate and had to destroy; it was out of his control.

He said he was sure, now that he had been able to talk about his problem, he would improve. We stayed together five more days. He never washed or changed his clothes, smelled awful and drank too much. On the fifth day he smashed even the table and the bed. I had gone to the outside toilet and heard the crashing. I hid and waited till he'd fallen asleep on the floor, then stealthily got my belongings and left.

That afternoon we had been to a small Greek fishermen's restaurant. After drinking retsina, the white wine flavoured by the pine resin used for sealing the barrels, and eating olive salad and crumbly white goat's cheese, all the men had got up to dance, first one, then two, then five. They had got the ladies to join them, pulling them in by extended handkerchiefs. An old fisherman had extended his hanky to me and, eager to learn new steps, I had joined the circle.

This was the most wonderful thing that had ever happened to me, this spontaneous Greek dancing. Never had I seen people express their happiness or forget their sorrows as the Greeks did with their *zirtakis*. I had experienced then the same deep-rooted joy of unity through a shared tradition as I'd felt at that first carnival in Basel. Here everyone seemed so relaxed, filled with that same happiness I'd envied Antony Quinn for in his film *Zorba the Greek*. At least here reality seemed as good as in a film. Carefree fun was a thing I was searching for, ever since my childhood. I'd been cheated out of it. It was to be found so rarely, and when I did find it, so often someone in my life would try to spoil it. Thinking this, I checked my tickets, made my way to the boat for Athens, and started my journey home to Basel.

Although, after our Greek trip, I found roses on my car windscreen, and letters begging me to come back and have confidence, I didn't dare renew my relationship with Roland.

I worked hard and concentrated on my career and Arlette. At this stage I'd had to move out of my flat and was again living at home, but as a result of Mother's usual scrubbing, cleaning and tidying frenzies, I was always in trouble. One day we got on; the next she wouldn't talk to me. I couldn't do a thing right. If I came home late, sneaking as quietly as I could up the creaking stairs, she'd worry about me not being serious enough and not getting enough sleep. If I stayed home, she'd grumble, I was using too much bath water, electricity, even her cleansing milk and cotton wool. About this time she began to put carpet-protectors on top of carpet-protectors on top of protectors for the carpet-protectors – and plastic on top of the lot! We were forever stumbling and tripping.

I was desperately looking for a flat.

I was depressed, feeling I didn't have the strength to pick myself up any more. When I ended up hiding away in my bed on free days, Mother made obvious noises of complaint, so I had to drag myself up.

I sat around, but she made me feel guilty, clattering with the dishes and the Hoover. Never was I able to crawl into a corner, so I did things so listlessly that we got on each other's nerves. Eventually I escaped to Claire's and told her the whole story.

'There are many people who are unable, or afraid, to love,' she told me. Real goodness wants to share, seeks to communicate, to grow together, but if a person's love is filled with guilt, it turns sour, turns into badness and becomes self-destructive. Roland must be full of things not worked through, full of rejection and guilt . . . like your mother.'

Claire was off into one of her lectures. I did listen, though, when she said, 'Not many of us can truly love. I once went to a Senior Citizens lecture on love. There we were told that love meant self-forgetfulness. Do we really want to focus on our partners, thinking only of his or her fulfilment and happiness? Or do we use them for fulfilling our own needs and satisfactions? Do we think it is love when we are using people?

'Olivia, you've told me so much about yourself that I know about the agonies of loneliness and the need to be loved, in you. You seem starved for emotional and spiritual answers. We are living in a pain-filled world, my dear. As long as one has pain, one focuses on self. If you bang your shin or head you won't be lovingly stroking your partner's head. So you see, as long as you hurt and your friends hurt, it is hard to stroke each other's hurts. We cannot become self-forgetting. We remain wrapped up in our egos and can't see the needs in the other. You will be unhappy and full of longing until you can resolve your problems, forgive and forget the past, so that it can dissolve away and not spoil your present life. But for everyone, *that* is the most difficult thing to learn in this obstacle-race called life.'

I began to feel like a heel. I'd never make it. I knew of many noble ways in which I wanted to grow, but I wasn't capable.

'Don't look so sad, Olly. You're on the best path because you ask and search and think. You haven't given up, and you care. You see, at the beginning of life, we are like little rosebuds. Delicate and closed. Only when we receive love and warmth can we open and grow and trust and develop all the talents within. If we don't have that, we can't develop normally.

'As a baby I had swallowed water of the womb. I couldn't keep down any food, so I was raised on herb tea. I cried so much, and made myself stiff, pushing out both arms against Mother, crying, day and night. She, with three small children and expecting another, soon resented me. I can't ever remember having hugged, or being hugged by, my mother. I never saw affection between her and Father. He was a quiet man, who just seemed to work and sleep. Mother took care of everything. I could tell that she was more at ease with my brothers and sisters. I always felt left out. Olly, I never learned how to love. And when I did, and was loved in return, I was so dependent, that when he left me for a younger woman fifteen years ago, I never got over it. It hurts still, and I miss him as if he left only yesterday. You never had stable affection. You were rejected over and over again. No wonder the dynamics of your personality are hindered in developing normally. You're doing a terrific job, though, and I admire the way you have had the courage to try and build up a relationship, again and again.'

'Claire, I hate sex. I'm terrified of it, every time, but I make myself do it. It's like wanting to learn to overcome the fear. I desperately want to become so-called "normal". Every time a relationship or something goes wrong, I feel I've failed, I'm in the wrong, and I lose the bit of self-confidence I had. I feel I'm such a miserable mother too, not able to give family warmth and love and security to Arlette, all over again.'

'It's always this vicious circle. If you don't learn the pattern of love and security, the pattern of how a family functions, how can you be able to pass it on? You're not to blame. You're trying to learn. I think you need good professional help.'

'I've tried that. It was awful! I never understood what the doctor was on about. And the silly tests. I didn't learn to know myself or how to change, or cope better. All they tell me is that I have an incredibly high IQ. So what?'

'There are may different psychological groups and approaches. Maybe you didn't find the one suitable for you? Look, stay here for tea. I'd like to talk to you. It hurts me to see you so sad. You have no reason to have so little confidence in yourself. I've seen you with Arlette. You're a wonderful mother and she adores you. It is just unfortunate that we women in Switzerland are at the mercy of a male-orientated and dominated society. In a few years you and Arlette would have been together. Besides, a more mature man than Tobias would never have risked damaging his child so drastically by insisting on such inhuman conditions. His pride and ego mean more to him than what his child and you are suffering. He will have to pay for it one day, but by then the damage to Arlette and you may be beyond repair. All you can do is to invest love into every moment you have her and for the rest, learn to be patient. If you work hard, and learn to settle and grow less restless, you can always take up the court on that provision about your situation changing.'

Claire gave me a quick hug.

'Try not to expect the change from the outside – or in a man! Try to work the change on the inside. Work on your own maturing. Learn to depend on yourself, and trust yourself. Once you can respect and trust yourself, you won't feel others have a right to put you down or judge you. As long as you go from one partner to the other, you'll lose yourself more and more. Only when you're ready to be a good partner and friend to yourself, are you ready to be a partner to someone else. I know you'll make it, because I can see what a valuable, lovely person you are. We've just got to dig you out from underneath all the rubble! Now, what would you like to eat?'

'Oh, Claire! I always feel so good here, with you. I sometimes fear being lectured, at first, but then when I relax and know that you really like me, I learn so much from you. I do love you. You're the most wonderful person I've ever met.'

'Don't exaggerate! I'm the one that's thankful for having met you. I love coming to your gym classes. You're so good at your work. See! There's something to be proud of. I've been to many different teachers and am thirty years older than you. Let me tell you, never have I found such variety. You come up with so many new and great ideas. It's such fun to work with you. And I love your dancing. Shall we work on a Hungarian one I learned, tonight?'

'Oh, yes! I'd love that.'

After a lovely light meal we got down to one of our dancing sessions, where we forgot the world and ourselves. I phoned Mother to say I was going to spend the night at Claire's. We put up her camp bed, on which I was too tired to feel how uncomfortable it was, and slept like a log.

It was always wonderful to have breakfast at Claire's apartment because she had an immense balcony on the top floor, and while we ate our croissants we watched her doves spluttering in the birdbath among her roof-garden plants. From here we could also see the ships gliding past on the Rhine. A 'Basel-belonging' feeling came over me and I felt grateful to have such a friend. Also at twelve I was going to pick up my daughter, who was a schoolgirl now.

Till noon I helped Claire tidy her big roof garden. Snipping away on her plants, I said 'I don't know how you do it. You work all week in that dingy little office you hate, walk home every lunchtime, work on your plants all weekend, and still find time to do so many interesting things.'

'I love my plants and the birds. They partly compensate for the forty years I have to work to get my pension and freedom at sixty-five. Only seven more years! This is where I tank up to be able to take it. I've always hated my office job, but after the war I had no choice. I had to help support my parents, now my sister and mother, but I've nearly got there. Just imagine the bliss! To be able to do with my days exactly what I want! I can't wait!'

I was impressed. I could never do it. And I realised that Claire was the same age as my mother.

I was off! Waving up to Claire who was bending over her balcony railing, I put down the roof of my Topolino. I felt free as if I had left all my troubles up there. I had a wonderful friend who loved me, whom I could trust and talk to. Her opinions were valuable, her thoughts of a quality I had missed since those discussions with Ivo. And now I had a whole weekend with Arlette in front of me.

Chapter Sixteen

I miss my little girl. I complete a solitary warm-up in my studio. Listlessly I make my tired body bend. This early Monday morning the room is cold, as *sou-sols* are. I start to prepare my lessons. The best person to get me into a better mood is Oscar Peterson, with *Night Train*. I plod through the room diagonally, improvising, jumping, sliding, combining steps, lunges and skips. On a mat, in the centre, I roll and tumble and stretch and contract. And suddenly creativity flows, my body becomes a willing instrument, no longer my own but a slave to music's rhythm. What rhythm can do for limbs and spirit! With the new routines and work-out to music, there is created the joy of wanting to share all this with my pupils, my clients, who come and pay, trusting me to make them feel good as well as become fit. As they arrive, each with an expectant 'Good morning', I no longer resent them for coming to take something from an empty shell, but am bursting to share, to give, to dip in to it all with them as though plunging into a never ceasing waterfall. . . .

It is twelve. The music has stopped and everyone has left. I feel tired, my previous sleepless night after taking Arlette back is now taking its toll. As I'm free this afternoon, till four, I decide to go and sit in the café round the corner, opposite the park. I'll eat there and prepare the lessons for later . . .

Engrossed with lessons, I was irritated by the noise of a revving motor in the garage next to the cafe. I saw a young man in overalls circling a Ferrari, tyres squealing. The rest of the garage hands were standing watching, obviously they didn't often have such a car to work on. The show stopped, and I worked on, only to be interrupted again by the same noise and stench. Furiously I looked up again and at the café table next to me a young man remarked, 'I wonder if that's absolutely necessary?' I looked at him.

'Actually, we know each other,' he said. 'I once met you, years ago. You lived in an apartment with your husband and baby. My name is Schmied. Sam Schmied.'

'I'm sorry, I don't remember.' I felt embarrassed, my mind a blank.

'We only met at an evening with many other people, but I always remembered you. I've seen you often, around Basel, since then.'

'I'm sorry. I never recognised you. I hope I didn't seem rude.'

He asked to join me at my table and as he stood up and I looked at him fully, it was, for a split second, as if a voice said, 'That's him. That's your future life, your fate, your destiny.' It was one of those uncanny things. Stupid imagination? Hopeful, momentary, easy-solution thinking? Or fantasy? I brushed these thoughts away as he sat down. He was not much taller than myself, wore glasses, had a huge moustache curling up at both sides and was of stocky stature. Solid and kind. Sensible. Some strange quality came over from him to me, as if I'd found a haven, a reliable place of rest in the storm. What on earth was I interpreting from all this?

'I'm a photographer. I have just been on a rather difficult assignment. I had to cart ladders and heavy equipment round a metal factory, to take shots for a new catalogue. It was stifling hot, I thought I'd have a cool beer before going up. I live on top of this house, my studio is up in the penthouse.'

'Sounds very interesting. I suppose a photographer must be very versatile?'

'True enough, but photography can be routine, boring at times, you know, the everyday bread and butter work, but there are highlights. Like next week I've got to go to North Africa to a place called Appollonia near Cyrene on an archaeological dig for the University of Michigan, so I'll be flying to Libya, all expenses paid. They pay extremely well, and that always helps when one is self-employed.'

'Wow! That's amazing. An archaeological dig? I bet it's fascinating to see things excavated and to be the first to see them after hundreds of years.'

'Yes, that's how I feel. And to have to take pictures of these things, before they are touched, and then after, when they've been restored. I'm really looking forward to it. University people from the States are always good to work with.'

'Have you done it before?'

'Yes. I was the expedition photographer for Michigan and Princeton Universities in the Sinai Desert in the old St Catherine monastery. We lived there for five months in all, and everyone became good friends. It was one of the most interesting times of my life.'

'What an opportunity!'

'It was. And afterwards I travelled all around Africa with one of the other photographers. It was great.'

'Well, you certainly have a tremendous job, and life. I envy people who can travel.'

'It doesn't happen that often. Anyway, tell me about yourself. How old's the baby now?'

'The baby is eight-and-a-half now. I'm divorced. I teach gymnastics. My studio's just around the corner.'

'Things must have changed a lot for you. That must be interesting work too.'

'Yes. I like it. Not much chance to travel though. I teach English, too, at the new evening school.'

'How come? Do you speak English well?'

'Yes. I went to school in Yorkshire for over four years. I prefer English to German and I like England better, too.'

'Why didn't you continue to live there?'

'Because one can't always do as one wants.'

'This is funny, because I prefer to speak English.' And in English with a strong American accent, he added, 'That's for sure! Let's speak English then. I haven't been able to for ages.'

I joined his laughter as I answered, 'Yes let's, I think this is great! You sound like a Yankee.'

'Would you like to come up and see my studio?'

I couldn't help replying, 'Said the photographer to the Bishop's wife, or in this case, to the gym teacher!'

And having found a mutual understanding in the more casual way of the English sense of humour, we laughed again.

'I'd love to see your penthouse,' I replied, 'but I still have two lessons to prepare. I'm free after, but I promised to bring some meat home for my Mother.'

'Is that far? Do you have to eat there too?'

Having become over cautious, I thought that I'd rather see his penthouse before going out with him, if he intended to ask me, because I hoped to learn more about him through his environment and the way he lived.

'After my two lessons, I could pop in to see you before I go to buy the meat and take it home. Mother lives out Binninger way. I think I'm expected to eat at home tonight.

I've just spent a weekend there with my daughter and my folks were helpful, so I feel I owe it to them. They are very special.'

We parted and I went to finish my preparations in my studio. The lessons went well. I worked out new exercises with balls finishing them with an extra daring flourish. I was greatly looking forward to seeing Sam again. I had to take the lift to the top of his house, then walk up another flight and step out on to the flat roof. There was an arrow, 'Photo Studio Sam Schmied.' A red door. I knocked. He opened it and beamed. A strong smell of chemical solutions hung in the air at the entrance, a smell that mingled with the aroma of coffee. To me the smell of coffee implied homeliness, but ever since my childhood I'd never been able to drink it without feeling sick. I was addicted to good, strong tea, still.

He offered me orange juice and we walked round.

I saw the whole of Basel. The view was splendid. Even the tile rooftops nearby were beautiful. A wide balcony ran all the way around the penthouse.

The photo studio part was huge. It was all white, with lamps, silver umbrellas, electronic flashes, huge rolls of coloured cardboard backdrops and curtains, ladders and tripods everywhere. Lost in a far corner, all by itself, was a low leather butterfly chair, in front of the television set. I imagined him sitting there, all alone. Off the studio led the living quarters with an enormous kitchen and a darkroom area with adjoining developing tables. In the living room he had his desk, business files and typewriter, to the right of which stood his bed, in the corner. There was a wall of shelves with the most splendid hi-fi equipment, records and books. A skull, baring its teeth, an Egyptian fez and other treasures stood and hung among old teddy-bears, a lopsided rabbit with one ear. Bits of torn out newspaper cuttings stuck by pins surrounded his desk. I saw the small boy and the man, in one. Again that whispering voice said, 'This is him.' Again I told myself not to be stupid.

Proudly he showed me little glass bottles blown from a blob of old glass which he had been given, by a monk in the old monastery. He also showed me Bedouin bracelets, tapestries, photographs, all cherished mementos. He seemed to be deeply affected by his time in the Sinai at the monastery. He loved the sacred old place, the way it was miles from anywhere, the rocks, sky and desert, the silence and the beauty. Also the architecture, the icons and the artefacts. He talked about the bell that brought him upright in bed with a start at four every morning and about the chants and prayers of monks and their booming sounds on the semandron. He chuckled about their all-too-human squabbling and burping and arguing.

He was impressed because there had been history everywhere he trod. His American friends, the professors, were fascinated and absorbed solely by Byzantinism. He told me about the day of bread-baking, the photography work, the rides up Mount Sinai on camels, the wadis, oases and gardens, about the supposedly Burning Bush and the Well of Moses, which were the reasons for the monastery's position and survival since the sixth century. The water had had to be boiled or disinfected before being fit for drinking. Tired of this business, Fred, one of his best friends, put water in a bottle, with a label, 'What's good enough for Moses is good enough for Fred!' He'd often say to Sam, 'Stop beating around the Burning Bush!'

I was having such an interesting time with Sam in his penthouse, at our first meeting there, that I completely forgot the time and had to rush away. I bought the best steak, costing me nearly all I'd earned that day, then drove home. Trying to forget Arlette's tears as she left me, I concentrated on the brunch and the lovely hours we'd spent this past weekend. I walked up to the house and as the door was open I could hear my mother's agitated voice on the phone. 'Now she had this doctor, director of the school, such a nice man in a good position, and she goes and spoils it all again. I just can't understand her. She's nearly thirty, and every time she meets someone it goes wrong. No wonder! She never makes her bed as neatly as she could, you know, or dries out the sink, or hangs her facecloth and towel out on the balcony to dry, like I tell her to and she always leaves her cup for me to dry, because she hates getting up, and is always in a rush. . . .' I must have stood there some minutes, going hot all over, till I suddenly flung the meat on the table and left, slamming the door. I ran back to the car. My mother! My own mother, talking like that about me behind my back. Again those petty complaints and accusations! Facecloth! Towel! I had hung them up where they belonged, in the bathroom.

That morning I'd rinsed and washed my cup, leaving it to dry on the side of the sink. I'd cleared everything away in spite of being in a hurry to get to work. Yet while rushing, I *knew* that something I'd do would get me into trouble. I always had that cramped, tense, feeling in Mother's house because whatever I did was never done how she wished. When Arlette was there, she couldn't do a thing wrong, and Mother and Andreas were tolerant and lovable as could be. Every three weeks I was convinced that they were wonderfully marvellous. I'd spoil them and try not to feel in their debt, but somehow I always felt guilty. I felt inferior, a loser who could never gain their full esteem.

I went to Claire.

I told her about the children's homes I'd been sent to, the way I had been made to have an abortion, and had felt I had to marry Tobias. The way they had made me sign everything, quick and easy, with a lawyer they'd chosen, resulting in my losing custody of Arlette. The way they'd never offered to take us in together after the divorce. The way I had always been pushed off to other people or homes to be brought up, the way Mother had often left me alone with Father and Frau Dresden, in Bradford, when Mother went to Basel, and the way she hadn't noticed what Father had been doing to me for years. The way I always felt I was blaming them, or was ungrateful and asking for too much. I told Claire how every time I'd wanted to talk over these things with my mother, she would say, 'Olly, don't take yourself so seriously,' and would get on with her cleaning and dusting.

Claire told me to ring up and say I was staying the night with her.

Mother was very cool. She said, 'I'm sorry you overheard me speaking to Laura, but I'm so concerned and worried about you. I can't die in peace unless you have a nice partner. It's out of love, that I worry.'

I said a low, 'Yes Mother. It's all right. Goodnight.'

Claire said it was 'sentimental blackmail'. She suggested I concentrate on my work, find my own apartment and prove that I could live a life of my own and have Arlette with me as soon as possible.

The next day a note on my Topolino windscreen from Sam cheered me up immensely. 'Hope you had enjoyable lessons. Please pop up for a min. Want to ask you something. Sam.'

So I popped up for a minute. Same smile, same smell behind the red door, same homely feeling.

'Would you like to come out to dinner with me tonight?' Since my experiences in the Fernsburg children's home, eating with people I didn't know well still had a horrible effect on me. Still I often couldn't eat at all. I always found myself in the dilemma of not wanting to hurt the person's feelings, not wanting to refuse their invitation because I liked company and meeting people but unable to explain further.

'It's very nice of you, but I'm never very hungry,' I said. 'A sandwich perhaps.'

Sam roared. 'You're the first girl that doesn't jump at being taken for a great big meal. Are you on a diet because of your job?'

'No. It's just because I'm a very small eater.' I burst into tears.

'What on earth's the matter? I ask you out to dinner and you cry. What am I, a monster?'

'I've had an awful row with my mother and it happens again and again, and every time I think everything's all right, and every time I trust her and relax, every darned time, it happens again. It's so awful and it's never stopped, as long as I can remember.'

'Well, if I were you, I'd look for a flat and live your own life.'

'I don't know if I can afford to, in the long run, for my clients are building up slowly and aren't very reliable. I'm a bit scared to commit myself with the prices of apartments and food and everything. I've only just paid off lawyers and furniture storage and car repairs. My studio has a high rent and I still need mats and more balls and hoops and things. You see, I only see my little girl at the weekends and therefore save up for holidays for her too. I just don't know how I'm going to handle it all.'

'Hold on!' Sam looked very understanding. 'Let's dry those tears, go out for a nice meal and wine, and you tell me all about it.'

I felt so reassured that I was fairly confident I'd be able to explain about my eating phobia, and he'd understand, so we went. He took me to the Peppermill, one of Basel's cosiest chalet-type restaurants. We sat down. Candles made our faces look familiar, as if we'd known each other for a long time. We ordered and I helped myself to small portions and managed to eat. Before the dessert, which I said I couldn't find room for, he bought me a rose from a girl who came round the tables, choosing the loveliest bloom from her basket.

After the meal, we walked around our city.

Suddenly he stopped and said, 'How would you like to look after my apartment, till I'm back from Africa?'

'You mean that you'd let me live there?'

'Yes. You'd get away from home, could look for a flat and at the same time water my plants and empty the letterbox.'

I was touched.

We went to his home so that he could show me what would need to be done.

From then on he had much to attend to. I had new clients and lessons and all too soon it was time he had to go. We hadn't had time for another meeting because he had many assignments and complicated paperwork to finish. We agreed I should come up on the eve of his departure to meet his landlord. Sam introduced me to this man and said he would leave him with a list of the things I needed to know and the key. I was to move in the day after. Sam had to leave early.

I could hardly wait. I'd had two flats since I'd been divorced. One was cheap, ugly and impracticable, with the loo in a backyard. After an attack of the flu and spending the cold winter nights out there with a bellyache and high fever, I'd gone back home. The second one had been too expensive, the rental going up every second month. Also I'd been frightened alone at night. I had never got used to it and hated coming home to an empty place. It drove me out, out anywhere, as much as possible. Just to sit amongst strangers; I felt just as lonely, and afterwards, I had to face coming home alone once more, just as I had done when I was married.

At least, in my own flat, every time I chose to go out, I had the hope of meeting someone. And now I had, I was determined to conquer my fears of living alone. I felt this an excellent opportunity.

Mother was still cool. She'd said she was sorry, which happened very rarely and was unusual, so we hugged and kissed and cried as I left with my books, my writing stuff and a few clothes. I'd be just round the corner from work.

I got the key. Mr Werner the landlord was nice, letting me know that he was there if needed. With a gut feeling of joy and expectation, I unlocked the red door. I walked into the studio, spread my arms, dropped the clothes and swung round and round and round. What space, what freedom, what privacy! Glorious! I went to the television set and saw a note on top.

'Switch on red button. Push here for programmes etc.' [All sorts of instructions followed on how to handle it.] Have a lovely time! See a good programme for me, too! Love, Sam.'

I smiled and turned it on, switched through all the channels then turned it off. In the kitchen was a note on the refrigerator: 'Hi, you little google-oogle! Have some yoghurt, some meat, some wine, some chocolates, anything you feel like. What's mine is yours. Enjoy yourself!' I felt hot inside. I hugged the note to my bosom as I walked into the living-bed-office-room. On the desk were roses. On the bed were chocolates. I cried. Then laughed out loud at the same time. I ran around the place like an idiot, to the bath, the loo and tiny spare room. Everywhere were little notes. Beside the toilet, beside the bath! What a man. Oh what a person! What a wonderful boy, man, I didn't know, just Sam!

I took a long time to put my things in their new places. Looking through his records I saw that he hardly had any classical ones and that his taste in music, in jazz, was great but much more modern than mine. There was a note on the record player too. 'My records are untouched by human hands!!'

I made a cup of tea, fried two eggs, peeled a carrot and an apple and sat down in front of the T.V. in the studio. It felt strange, and the sound echoed in the big room. I felt the old familiar fear creep up on me, so I went into the small living room and closed all the doors. I had a bath, then hurried and snuggled into his bed where I read and ate chocolates. I'd invite Claire over for the next evening, I decided as I went to clean my teeth. I read till I dropped off to sleep. Suddenly a loud clatter woke and terrified me. It took all my courage to go and find out that his pan-lids, on a rack in the kitchen, had fallen off the wall. In the morning I felt tired but proud and contented. I went to work and loved running home for lunch and a shower. The next evening Claire came. I cooked for us and showed her round proudly, indicating Sam's notes to me. As she looked, she said, 'He seems to be a very original personality. I've never seen such an interesting mixture of knick-knacks, treasures and ordinary things mixed together. I love his taste. He must have a great sense of humour.'

'He has.' I said. 'He's very, very kind.'

After Claire left, I sat down to write to Sam. I couldn't thank him enough and tell him about everything around me, couldn't wait for his reply. I felt happy, as if Christmas stood in front of the door.

My next weekend with Arlette, in the new place, was great. We played with balls on the floor in the studio. We went to the gym to jump and make up new dances. We ran to the shops and down to the Rhine, for now we were in the 'small Basel' area. We had a restaurant just down below in our house. It was all new and exciting. Being alone for a change, we did many things together, just the two of us. We dreaded the time as it got nearer to six o'clock on Sunday night.

Sam wrote. He wished me a good time amongst his things and told me of all the old head masks, chariot shields and coppers coming to light for the first time in centuries. Of how exhilarated he felt when he had to take a picture. He wrote sensitive descriptions of the sunsets, the dawns, the space and the beauty. He said he was looking forward to seeing me. I couldn't understand why a person like him was not married.

Sam came back. I prepared to move out, but he said I needn't. Old fears and suspicions! He said I could live in the little spare room till I found a suitable flat and could stay as long as I wanted. Did I want this? What did I want? It seemed too easy. Would I be expected to pay a price? 'Can I pay the rent?' I asked. 'No. Just do a bit of cooking if you feel like it. I have a cleaning woman here, twice a month. You're welcome.'

I started to look for a cheap flat, but very half-heartedly. And then, all too soon, everything became too normal. I wanted to adore him as 'Mr Wonderful', have a good time and relationship but all from a safe distance.

I didn't know how disturbed and mixed up I still was. Neither I nor my mother nor Sam realised how I had failed to get over the deep harm of my childhood experiences nor were we aware of the additional hurt and damage my failed marriage had rendered. Also our mother-daughter relationship was cutting me into bits. I was a smiling but grieving, sick and emotionally crippled person with no inner peace. I'd cling to people or pretend I didn't need them, all in my efforts to build a life I perceived as normal. I kept wondering why my attempts did not succeed. Underneath I had strange thoughts, fears, aims and ideas but at surface level I tried to talk and think and act like others did. All the time I wondered why these 'others' seemed to function so easily. It was exhausting, always struggling to keep up appearances, trying to be the same as others while hating myself because I was different, running against the tide.

There was such chaos inside me, such rejection and self-condemnation. The more I had to flirt, and charm, and prove that I was the best, the most intelligent, the most efficient, the prettiest and the one worth loving, the more I knew what a failure I was. I had to work so hard to convince people of my worth, I was forever tired and near killed myself in the attempts. My constant fear was that I'd be discovered to be the rotten, empty, soiled, superficial 'nothing' I believed I was. A person unworthy of love or acceptance, a phoney.

I was convinced everyone would abandon me eventually, so it became important that I dropped them before they dropped me. But maybe just once I might be able to make it. If once, someone would love me, even if I was a naughty, bad girl, then maybe I could be better. But no, that would not really be possible because I didn't understand the simplest things. I couldn't be tidy, easily. I was afraid to sleep alone; couldn't even eat with strangers, had difficulty in learning and remembering things or concentrating. I had awful trouble trying to read politics, so couldn't really join in good conversations, but just bluffed my way along as if I understood, but inside I felt incredibly stupid. I could shimmer for a while like a butterfly but I knew that at any moment people would see through me for I just couldn't keep up a so-called normal, everyday life. I hated it. I needed change and excitement. Life had too much to offer for a person to get stuck in a groove. I was too interested in too many interesting things. No! It was them! They were all phoneys, hypocrites, squares; boring, ordinary, stupid, dull people not worth loving. Not I. It was them! They'd probably never suffered and were judging me.

And now I was already wondering why Sam expected me to like such an unromantic life. He wasn't making any attempts to woo me. After three weeks of cooking and cleaning for him I decided to go. It was the 'taken-for-granted-ness' I didn't like. What a life! He'd take me out to a film but then go straight home. I loved to see and be seen. He saved his money and always wanted to go home for a drink. For me, tea in a restaurant, where I didn't have to prepare and clear up afterwards, tasted so much nicer. He was stingy and a bore I thought. I decided to find a flat. I worked hard like a housewife and earned a living. The old marriage fear came back. What would one talk about, all evening? He didn't seem to know how to communicate. It was good one moment and boring the next. I was teaching in seven different places which added pressures, and seemed forever to be rushing, teaching, shopping, cooking and cleaning.

One of my English pupils said she had a room to let in an attic. I decided to tell Sam. 'I'd like to invite you to a film and then to a meal and a drink, tonight.' I said.

'No, it's O.K.' he replied. 'I'll invite you to a film, then let's come home. I don't like sitting in smoky, noisy places afterwards.'

'Oh Sam, just this once! Please! I love going out and it's so lovely to sit in a nice restaurant and see people. I do love it so. We could feel part of it. You know, it's our town and there are many interesting places and people. I'd like to introduce you to some of my friends, too.'

'No. A film yes, but then let's go home.'

I decided that I didn't want that way of life, and thought him domineering and stubborn. The next day I told him I'd found a flat, and I moved out.

I missed him.

After two weeks I phoned to see how he was. He asked to take me to see a play at the theatre. We went together and afterwards he took me straight home to my new address and drove off. I was furious. He said he didn't want to pretend he was any different from the way he was. If I liked him, fine. If I didn't, fine too. He said he more than liked me. I was baffled.

I thought about it all and weighed up Sam's values against mine. I missed him and all his kind ways. I phoned once more and told him so.

'I never asked you to go. You're welcome to come back whenever you want,' he said.

'Couldn't you say you missed me, too?'

'I could.' He laughed.

I went back.

Chapter Seventeen

Bradford
April 1980

Dear Olivia,

How are you? It's always so lovely to hear from you. Even though we don't write more than two or three times a year, it is marvellous how we've kept in contact over all this time since the death of your father.

After all your ups and downs and struggles, I'm so glad to hear that you have found a nice husband, built a house and had a second daughter. You really deserve to be happy after all you've been through. I think the way you have come through life is great and you are to be congratulated. Many girls with a better start haven't managed to cope so well. I often wondered what would have happened if you could have stayed in England. Anyway, everything you describe now sounds wonderful. . . .

Because I know how you always miss Yorkshire, I am enclosing some pressed bluebells and heather from the moors.

I pray it will stop raining soon. We are all fed up with it. Hoping to hear from you before too long.

Yours,
Ivy Killarney

Auckland, New Zealand
September 1984

Dear Miss Killarney,

How are you these days? Sorry I haven't written for ages, but there has been another drastic change in my life. We emigrated from Switzerland to New Zealand!

Change! Always change, when all I ever longed for were roots, to have a warm, confidence-inspiring 'mother hen', and my own family and loved ones round the table. I must have been the world's worst emigrant! I cried all the way from Basel to Auckland! It was here, homesick and unsettled, that I found my old wounds reopening. Suddenly I was in English-speaking surroundings and the theme on radio, television, in newspapers, books and films, was incest. They claimed that every third or fourth child was sexually molested at some stage in life. Out of pain, loneliness and the need to help others, because I know how such experiences affect a whole lifetime, I began to write. It helped me stay sane while trying to find my own identity.

I talked to a child welfare psychiatrist about incest victims. I told her how my second husband saved me from total self-destruction, because he had patience and understanding. He kept on loving me even during those episodes where I had the compulsion to 'test' him to see if he would love me even if I was 'a bad girl' and it's only thanks to his faith in me, though I was crippled and full of hang-ups, that I have made it. Everybody feels sorry for the 'little-girl victims', but who thinks of the partners and children of these victims of traumatic childhood experiences? I often felt devastated by everything my Arlette and Sam and many others had to suffer, because of my past and its consequences. I had so many invisible demons on my back and only now, far from Basel, can I speak, write and think about it all clearly and without guilt feelings.

We now have a wonderful marriage and a fabulous family life. As you know, we've worked hard on this over the years but have come to realise that truly, the more one gives into a relationship the more one gets in return. At times it was very, very hard and we thought we'd never make it.

Belinda is lovely and still at an age where she enjoys baking a cake with me, while listening to her pop-songs on the radio. We have a little dance in the kitchen while at it. She's making great progress with her guitar and singing, and is breeding mice and dwarf rabbits. She builds cages and saws and hammers away for hours. She still thinks that school interferes with her time of making things and doing things! She has blue eyes and blonde curls, is strong-willed, self-confident, very independent and has a great sense of humour. She speaks English like a Kiwi. We are very close. I teach jazz-gymnastics, French, German and English. Here, where anyone can have their own pony, I still can't believe that my life-long wish has come true. I have a horse of my own. Melissa-Melody-Jane! I can see how it has taught me to overcome fear and not be manipulated but put my will over something stronger.

So many wonderful things are possible and open to everyone here in New Zealand. Anyone can open a restaurant or go to university, even oldies! I went to creative writing classes at the university and came first with a short story. All my inferiority complexes are starting to melt away in the South Pacific sun.

My Sam is very happy. As an advertising photographer working alone in Switzerland, he decided to get out of the 'rat race' before it killed him. I thought it was his mid-life crisis and that he'd get over it but he didn't. He is now a confirmed 'beach-bum' and loves fishing! His book about the St Catherine's monastery is out in four languages and he's sold over 30,000 copies. So as you can realise, we feel we've really made it to paradise. I can't get over the sea view. Our bedroom seems to be hanging over the cliff. Coming from my land-locked little country, I felt I needed to go to bed with a crash-helmet and parachute for the first few months.

Now that I've got over my worst homesickness and guilt feelings, I am beginning to settle down. Talking about guilt, after I finished my book, I found a publisher who is enthusiastic. It has taken me four years to put the book together because I had to learn better English and I can't spell for toffee. Now that it's all happening, I sometimes wonder if I have a right to do this, because of Mother. I'm sorry that so many nice memories seem to be buried under the rubble. It's still the same. For a while our letters are fine then suddenly I get one full of reproaches, and Mother still manages to upset and hurt me deeply. I try to justify myself and we end up quarrelling and hurting each other more. I still don't understand how it happens again and again. And yet, I had so many lovely times with Mother and Andreas and Arlette. Holidays where we laughed together in places like Vienna, Salzburg and Germany and France. Times of carefree love and fun, where we could forget, but the demons of the past never let go, never stayed away for long.

One memory keeps on coming back: once on coming home from school in Bradford, I found Mother knitting brown finger-gloves for me which she lined and embroidered with yellow wool to match my school uniform. I didn't know she could knit. My hands were always chafed and sore from the wind when I was twelve. I was so delighted that I never got over leaving them behind on the bus and never finding them again.

Another memory that haunts me is the time Arlette had anorexia. Here I keep seeing her sad face at our parting. I try not to think about it nor to see in my mind Mother's white face and pain-filled eyes as our friends had to tear us out of each other's arms, before we emigrated.

Miss Killarney, mine is a compassionate book, leading from dark despair to the light. I'm trying to reach Mother and Arlette with it, trying to explain, but probably doing it badly, as I seem to have a hard time winning there. Mother has had chronic shingles since I left and I'm very, very sorry for her. But we are unable to communicate in harmony for any length of time on a deeper level, so I've stopped trying in order to survive although I feel bad about it. I just talk about the weather. I am learning, at last, that I need not feel guilty when I'm happy and that I have a right to live a life of my own. I was conditioned and manipulated for too long. Thanks to Sam, I feel I've at last broken free.

While writing this book, a vital question cropped up and I'm surprised it took me so long to think of it!

I never understood what happened. Why, after I told you everything, didn't you come and get him? Why was he left to nearly kill me, kill Mother, and finally to kill himself? Why didn't anybody *do* anything? Why? Why didn't the police confront him and take him away?

Miss Killarney, I think I've managed to come to terms with my life and now feel balanced and much more mature, but only because I never gave up. It's taken energy, and courage, believe me, because it's been a mammoth task. Please. I'm nearly fifty! I now want to put it all out of my mind, so I beg you to help me with the answer to my final question. . . .

God bless you.

Olivia, with love.

Bradford
19 November, 1985

Dear Olivia,

Thank you for the long letter. I was pleased and interested to hear all about your new life in New Zealand.

I will pray for an improvement in the relationships between you and your mother, and your grown-up daughter. Only time can heal. As Arlette grows older and more mature, she will be able to understand you better. It's terrible how unhappy childhoods such as yours will go on affecting the future and harm not only the later lives of the victims but also that of any children they might have. It's a vicious circle. But now I'm sure there will be an end to all this in your life.

I'm glad to hear your book is now completed, but I'm afraid I cannot say exactly this long afterwards, why we did what we did at the time you told me what had happened. The only thing I can think of is that my senior officer would need to have all the information that I obtained in writing, and then have to go to the chief constable and then to the magistrates, because the police would need a warrant to arrest your father. You see, we only had the word of a little girl . . .

Father do you know what you did to me when

You murdered my innocence
Father, there and then?
Killed it in one night, Father,
When I was ten.

You found room in me
Father, later and then
It hurt like hell, Father,
When I was ten.

I found no room for me in you
Father, as you blew up my bridge, then
From childhood to adulthood, Father,
When I was ten.

How could I grow mature,
Father, building on abuse and tears,
How could I learn responsibility and choice, Father,
In those ten and four more years?

When I held a book,
Father, in front of my face to pretend it wasn't true.
You split my body, Father,
And my personality in two.
And when you dragged me from my secret hiding places,
You, father, broke my will and self, for always too.

You are dead now,
Father, leaving me unprepared for a journey of pain
Trying to erase at every crossroad
Memories of you and mother from my damaged brain.

Trying to become a normal wife and mother
Trying to forget you, rough between my legs,
Trying desperately not to feel so childish and so different
Even when I hang the washing up with pegs

for

Every little deed became a struggle,
Father, using up my whole life's energy, now as then,
When you chose to murder off my innocence, Father,
Once upon a time, when I was ten.

You found room in me,
Father, when I was ten
I am fifty now, still cry and hurt since then,
Since then, my Father, yes, since then,
For you arrested me, into staying always ten.

Chapter Eighteen

I have just sat down and cried because my father died. He died thirty-six years ago. In one month I'll be fifty. I could cry about him for the first time after reading Sandra Butler's book, 'Conspiracy of Silence: The Trauma of Incest.' (Volcano Press, 1978) She doesn't only write about the victims but about the mothers, the family and the aggressors. Through this I started to see my father as a human being for the first time. I suddenly saw how he must have placed the barrel of his pistol in his mouth and pulled the trigger and I started to think about what he must have gone through to do a thing like that. To actually, willingly decide to splatter his brains all over the mattress he had so often abused me on, the mattress with the washed, pink stains I saw at the age of fourteen. I desperately searched my mind for a nicer memory and I saw him sitting in front of the scullery fireplace, hammering a pattern with a nail and hammer into the wooden music box he made for me one Christmas. I decided I would hang on to that good picture of him. For the first time I wondered what sort of pressures he'd been under, if he was happy at work, and if he ever felt loved or understood. I wasn't attempting to excuse what he did to me, because he was the responsible adult and parent, but I asked myself if he needed a bit of warmth, and closeness, and power, and stole it, like a sick kleptomaniac, from me.

As I sat there, crying, feelings of compassion and love suddenly swept away that old frozen heaviness inside and I understood things that I never understood before. It was as if I'd always been retarded. As if I could never grow and mature or get in touch with reality, because I was using all my energy just to stay alive and try to cope. I exhausted myself, groping in the dark, copying lives, copying what I thought one was supposed to do. I didn't know I had the right to make decisions, didn't know I had the right to live my own life the way I wanted to and not the way I heard my mother and father speak to me inside my mind and body. I seemed always to be standing on the periphery of blurred edges, seeing surfaces but gaining no ideas of what made life, and particularly human relationships, work the way they did.

After this awakening, I began to reach out. I met other incest survivors. The confrontation with them was like a bang on the head that jolted me out of a sort of amnesia. My own suffering grew smaller in comparison. I could not bear to think what it must have been like to become pregnant by one's own father as a child. My heart went out to women who had been penetrated at the age of three and four, or younger, feeling as if they were 'cut in two, from top to bottom, with a knife,' left with mutilated genital parts and pain for the rest of their lives. One woman's virginity was taken with a hairbrush at the age of six; one woman heard of another's daughter in Germany who died after a bottle was pushed up her and the vacuum pulled out her insides. . . . All I could do was hold the hands of these sister victims and silently cry with them.

I still feel resentment towards my mother at times, then I feel failure because of this. However, I have learned that I have no right to judge or condemn anyone. I have hurt many people because of my childhood, and I can seldom know what other people went through in their early lives to make them act the way they do now. Even after a good childhood, people have to learn to be caring; everyone needs to study relationships and the art of successful communication throughout adult life. It's the art of good living and loving and it's hard to learn! And maybe that's all we're here for. If I harbour hate or resentment, I only hurt myself and stop myself from growing. As my main aim is to achieve inner peace, grow wiser, happier, more loving, caring and understanding, I have decided not to stand in my own way. For that is all we do if we don't work through a difficult area, forgive and forget, try harder and move on.

> There is no fear in love; but perfect love casts out fear because fear involves pain and torment. But he who fears has not yet become perfect in love.
>
> *1. John. 4/18*